PUTTING DOWN ROOTS

PUTTING DOWN ROOTS

FATHER JOSEPH MUZQUIZ AND THE GROWTH OF OPUS DEI

—— 1912–1983 ——

John F. Coverdale

 Scepter

Copyright © 2009, Scepter Publishers, Inc.
P.O. Box 211, New York, N.Y. 10018
www.scepterpublishers.org

Printed in the United States of America

ISBN-13: 978-1-59417-081-2

First printing, October 2009
Second printing, November 2009

Library of Congress Cataloging-in-Publication Data
Coverdale, John F., 1940-
    Putting down roots : Father Joseph Muzquiz and the growth of Opus Dei, 1912-1983 / John F. Coverdale.
        p. cm.
    ISBN 978-1-59417-081-2 (alk. paper)
        1. Opus Dei (Society)–History–20th century. 2. Opus Dei (Society)–United States–History–20th century. 3. Muzquiz, Joseph, 1912-1983.
        I. Title.
    BX819.3.O68C675 2009
    267'.182092–dc22
    [B]

                                                                2009035361

CONTENTS

NOTE TO THE READER ON SOURCES

This brief biography rests primarily on two groups of sources: 1) Father Muzquiz's papers including his correspondence with St. Josemaría Escrivá and 2) the written recollections of many people who knew him. I have quoted frequently from both because the actual words of Father Muzquiz and of the people who knew him are richer and more informative than a paraphrase.

When a quotation is from Father Muzquiz, that will be obvious from the text. I considered using footnotes to give the names of the persons whose recollections I quote. On further reflection I realized that since readers would not recognize the names, footnotes would only encumber the text without providing useful information. I decided, therefore, to omit them.

If a reader is interested in the source of a particular statement, inquiries can be directed to *coverdale.john@gmail.com.*

INTRODUCTION

Late in the afternoon of February 17, 1949, Father Jose Luis Muzquiz,[1] a thirty-six-year-old Spanish priest, arrived in New York aboard a TWA Super Constellation. He was accompanied by Sal Ferigle,[2] a physics graduate student. Neither of them spoke much English, and between the two of them they had only a few dollars to their name. They had come to begin the apostolic activities of Opus Dei in the United States. Today Opus Dei is a well-known personal prelature of the Catholic Church whose founder, St. Josemaría Escrivá, was canonized by Pope John Paul II, but in 1949 only a handful of Americans had ever heard of it.

Thirty-four years later, on Sunday June 5, 1983, only a few weeks before his sudden death, Muzquiz joined a thousand American members and friends of the Work—as Opus Dei is popularly called—in an auditorium at Hunter College in New York for an informal meeting with the Prelate of Opus Dei, Monsignor Alvaro Del Portillo. As he hugged Muzquiz, Del Portillo commented, "You have to thank God and feel great joy seeing that the Work has put down deep roots in the United States."

Today, many people throughout the United States and in other countries pray to Father Joseph, as he was called in this country, and pray that one day the Church will declare him a saint. Readers of this book will learn why.

---

1. Like most Spaniards, on more formal occasions and in official documents Muzquiz used both his father's and his mother's last name, thus being Jose Luis Muzquiz de Miguel. Although Muzquiz is accented in Spanish, he did not accent it in the United States or when writing in English. I have respected his choice.

2. His full name was Salvador Martínez Ferigle, but in the United States he was known as Sal Ferigle and after his ordination in 1957 as Father Sal.

PART I

Spain

—— 1912–1949 ——

∼ I.

YOUTH AND FIRST
CONTACTS WITH OPUS DEI

JOSE LUIS MUZQUIZ WAS BORN ON OCTOBER 14, 1912, in the city of Badajoz in the southwestern corner of Spain, close to the Spanish-Portuguese border. He was the first child of the former María de Miguel, the twenty-three-year-old daughter of a prominent Badajoz physician and landowner, and Miguel Muzquiz, a thirty-year-old career army officer. Miguel Muzquiz's father, an engineer, had emigrated to Cuba with his family after he lost his possessions as a result of a civil war in Spain. He had died in Cuba when Miguel was thirteen. His widow had returned to Spain with her six children. Miguel would have liked to become a professor, but decided to attend the military academy instead so as to help the family economically. He met and married María while stationed in Badajoz.

The Muzquizs, an affectionate couple who got along well together, were unusually independent by the standards of the time. During the first part of the family's summer vacations, Miguel, who had become a baseball fan during his youth in Cuba, would travel alone to attend the Spanish baseball championships before joining the rest of the family in Badajoz. María for her part went to the movies unaccompanied by Miguel, although it was unusual for married Spanish women to attend movies without their husbands. Both attended Mass and received communion daily, but normally they went to church separately.

While Jose Luis was still an infant, his father obtained an appointment as professor of languages at the military academy and the family moved to Toledo, fifty miles southeast of Madrid. There Muzquiz began his education in the public school. Although he was first in his class, his father felt he didn't study enough.

The Muzquizs spent their summer vacations in María's family home near Badajoz where Jose Luis played cops and robbers with his cousins and enjoyed life in the countryside. His letters to his father display a normal boy's interest in farm animals and in automobiles, which were still fairly rare in Spain. When he was fourteen, his father resigned his commission in the army and moved the family to Madrid where he took a position as a teacher in a Jesuit high school. That same year Jose Luis' only sister, Sagrario, was born. Although he was an affectionate older brother and looked out for his sister, because of their age difference they were, in her words, "more like two only children than like brother and sister."

Muzquiz studied science in the high school where his father taught and earned top grades in all subjects. He joined the school's religious association, and headed a group of students who taught catechism to younger students in one of the poorer neighborhoods of Madrid. One of his classmates recalls him as "one of the tallest students in the class, friendly, unusually mature, self-controlled, and pious."

After graduating from high school in 1928, Muzquiz decided to study civil engineering, a subject taught only in Madrid's Special School of Engineering of Highways, Canals, and Ports, one of the most prestigious university-level institutions in Spain and one of the most selective. Students had to pass a rigorous entrance exam in mathematics and other subjects at a level well beyond what was taught in high school. It was common to spend three, four, or even five years in private academies preparing for the exam. After only two years, Muzquiz won admission to the school in a year in which more than nine hundred applicants vied for thirty places. He was one of only two students in his year to be admitted less than three years after graduating from high school.

On the basis of his scores on the entrance exam, Muzquiz entered the engineering school as the second-ranked student. He told his father that he had no intention of trying to displace the first-ranked student, who was a good friend. He studied every day but not very long, often while walking around the house humming to himself and eating a late afternoon snack that left the house full of crumbs. He did not cram for exams and at times went to a party on the night before an exam. To earn spending money, he tutored students in mathematics. Occasionally he played practical jokes on his fellow students. After a field trip to Soria, for example, he sent a classmate a bogus letter supposedly from a young woman they had met during the trip.

A tall, handsome, athletic student with excellent professional and financial prospects and a pleasant character, Muzquiz enjoyed an active social life and had lots of friends among girls his age, but no serious girl friend. He belonged to a tennis club, where he often played with his cousins. On Sundays he liked to ski with several friends in the mountains near Madrid, often returning late. He spent the summers of 1932 and 1933 in England learning English.

During his college years Muzquiz, who was involved in Catholic Action, heard of Father Josemaría Escrivá, a young diocesan priest who was working with students at a recently founded Academy called DYA. Rumor had it that some of the students involved with Escrivá planned to dedicate themselves completely to God in celibacy while continuing to live in the world and practice their professions. This struck Muzquiz as "something odd and strange that could not succeed." He shared the generally held belief that those who wanted to dedicate themselves to God had to enter the seminary or better yet join a religious order and separate themselves from the world.

During the school year 1934–35, Muzquiz taught math to street urchins as a volunteer at the Porta-Coeli asylum. A young man named Laureano, an employee there, mentioned Muzquiz to Escrivá. Escrivá had been praying for Muzquiz for several years, ever since Muzquiz's aunt had told him about her talented nephew. He asked Laureano to arrange a meeting. Muzquiz agreed to stop by to see Escrivá, partly out of curiosity and partly because Laureano had gone to the trouble of setting up a meeting, but he had no intention of going beyond a simple courtesy visit.

They met in late 1934 or early 1935. Muzquiz's first impression was of "a cheerful young priest who spoke about God and immediately won my confidence." He was taken from the start by the warmth of Escrivá's greeting, and struck moments later when Escrivá said that he had prayed a great deal for him. Above all, however, he was impressed when Escrivá added with obvious conviction, "There is no greater love than Love. All other loves are little loves." The words, he sensed, "came from the depths of his soul, a soul in love with God." Although Muzquiz had dealt with many priests, none had ever spoken to him in this fashion. Forty years later, talking to a group of members of Opus Dei, he commented that he had never forgotten Escrivá's words about Love and hoped that they would also remember them.

Escrivá explained that the aim of the DYA Academy was to give deep Christian formation to students. Taking Muzquiz into his confidence, he said that although people understood the acronym DYA to stand for *Derecho y Arquitectura* [Law and Architecture], the two principal subjects taught at the academy, "we understand it to mean *Dios y Audacia* [God and Daring]."

Escrivá told Muzquiz about a series of classes he was giving at DYA to help students develop a solid interior life of prayer and union with God in and through their studies and other normal daily activities. The classes, which he called "circles," were different from the meetings of Catholic groups at the university with which Muzquiz was familiar. Rather than endless discussions that led nowhere, they were short practical sessions to which students came to learn and to put into practice what they learned. Escrivá said that there were openings in two circles for people of Muzquiz's age and academic interests. "Which of the two works better for you?" he asked. "One of the times," Muzquiz recalled many years later, "didn't work at all. The other wasn't convenient, but I picked that one and began to attend."

The circles met every week for a little less than an hour. Escrivá gave a talk on some aspect of Christian life, followed by an examination of conscience and some spiritual reading. The message was that God had called each of the participants—and indeed every Christian—to love Him wholeheartedly and to love others and to try to bring them closer to Him. This call to sanctity and apostolate did not imply becoming a priest or joining a religious order. God was calling them to sanctify themselves and to be apostles in the midst of the world through their daily work, which at the moment consisted above all in studying. They needed to learn to sanctify their studies, to make them an encounter with God, to turn them into prayer and sacrifice. And to do that, they needed to work well, to take their studies seriously, and to use their time well.

They also needed to become what Escrivá described as "men of prayer." This involved not only going to Mass and saying the Rosary and other vocal prayers, but setting aside some time each day for mental prayer. Escrivá presented mental prayer not as a complicated exercise but as a simple, childlike face-to-face conversation with God. Two points from his book *The Way* capture the tone and substance of his advice on mental prayer: "You say that you don't know how to pray? Put yourself in the presence of God, and once you have said, 'Lord, I don't know how to pray!' rest assured that you have begun to do so;" and "You write: 'To pray is to talk with God. But about what?' About what? About Him, about yourself: joys, sorrows, successes and failures, noble ambitions, daily worries, weaknesses! And acts of thanksgiving and petitions: and Love and reparation. In a word: to get to know him and to get to know yourself: 'to get acquainted!'"

Mental prayer would be the foundation for a contemplative life in the midst of the hustle and bustle of ordinary daily life. It would make it possible to live in the presence of God, turning to him frequently during the day, with short petitions, acts of adoration, thanksgiving, and reparation and resting in his fatherly providence.

Another recurring topic was the role of sacrifice in the Christian life. Starting with Christ's invitation to take up the cross and follow Him, Escrivá stressed that without a spirit of sacrifice his listeners would never come close to Christ. God was asking of them not spectacular penances but constancy and generosity in small everyday sacrifices: getting up promptly in the morning, punctuality, making good use of their time, studying in depth the subjects they found less interesting, smiling in the face of daily annoyances, accepting setbacks with good humor, temperance in food and drink.

Escrivá gave his teaching on the importance of prayer and sacrifice a practical thrust by asking the students to pray and offer sacrifices for specific intentions. Frequently he would ask whom they knew who might benefit from attending the circle. Once they settled on the name of someone who seemed a good candidate, he would urge them not simply to invite the fellow but to pray and offer sacrifices to win the graces he would need to respond favorably. Other times he would ask their prayers for DYA's needs: to complete the oratory or to find a new, larger location.

From the beginning, Muzquiz realized that the formation he received at DYA was deeper than what he had received in other Catholic activities. Previously he had not understood that laymen were called to lead an interior life of prayer and sacrifice. He was profoundly impressed by "meeting people who had and talked about interior life, a world that till then I knew nothing about."

INITIALLY ESCRIVÁ CONFINED HIMSELF to helping Muzquiz and the other participants in the circle deepen and develop their Christian lives without talking with them about Opus Dei. Escrivá had founded Opus Dei on October 2,1928. On that day he had seen that God wanted there to be in the Church people who would respond wholeheartedly to God's call to seek holiness in ordinary life. They would dedicate their own lives to God, living out that vocation in their work and spreading the joyful message that God calls every Christian to the fullness of holiness.

Eventually Opus Dei would be approved by the Church as a worldwide personal prelature with its own prelate, clergy, and lay people, some of whom would dedicate themselves to God in apostolic celibacy but the majority of whom would be married. In the mid 1930s, however, it had neither requested nor received any legal recognition. From the point of view of canon law, it was nothing more than an informal group of people each of whom had made a personal decision to embrace apostolic celibacy, to try to live an intense spiritual life under Escrivá's guidance, and to carry out what he described as an "apostolate of friendship and confidence" with colleagues, relatives, and friends primarily through their example and personal conversation.

Under these circumstances, Escrivá felt no need to talk about Opus Dei except with people whom he thought God might be calling to form part of it. One day Escrivá told Muzquiz that some of the students at DYA had decided to dedicate their lives entirely to God, living apostolic celibacy in the midst of the world while continuing to carry out their professional work. "I'm glad to hear that," Muzquiz responded, "but that's not for me." Without insisting further, Escrivá replied, "I'm telling you so that you will pray for us."

On another occasion, Escrivá told Muzquiz that the director of DYA, Ricardo Fernández Vallespín, was planning to go to

Valencia to start a residence like DYA. Muzquiz was impressed that a young architect with a good job in Madrid would be willing to give it up to go start a student residence in Valencia, but he still felt no inclination toward that degree of dedication. He enjoyed dances and parties and had no sense that God was calling him to give them up. He thought Opus Dei was only a passing phenomenon that Escrivá had thought up and that would fail when he died or grew tired.

Muzquiz graduated in January, 1936 as the second-ranked student in his class. In the midst of the Depression, it was not easy even for a top-ranked graduate of a prestigious school to find a job. Half a year later, Muzquiz had an offer of a position in the port of Alicante, but no definite start date. He decided to make a novena to Our Lady, asking for her help. At the time, most Spanish Catholics thought of novenas as florid devotions for pious old ladies. In one of the circles, however, Escrivá had explained that a novena could be a sober, manly practice: a nine-day period of greater closeness to Mary, marked not by external ceremonies but by saying daily some prayer to her and offering some sacrifice in her honor. The day Muzquiz finished his novena, he received a letter from a friend telling him that the port director had gone on vacation, so nothing was going to happen for at least a few weeks. He suggested that Muzquiz take advantage of the time to travel. He took the suggestion and decided to go to Germany to improve his German as well as to visit sites that were interesting from the civil engineering point of view.

~ **2.**

THE SPANISH CIVIL WAR

MUZQUIZ LEFT FOR GERMANY A WEEK before the outbreak of the Spanish Civil War in July 1936. Being out of the country may well have saved his life. Many young professional men, especially those who were active in Catholic Action or known as Catholics, were assassinated in the early months of the Civil War in Madrid. Among those who lost their lives were many of Muzquiz's best friends. Looking back on the events, he attributed his own survival to the protection of the Blessed Virgin.

As soon as he heard about the outbreak of the Civil War, Muzquiz left Germany. The principal points of entry to Spain were within the Republican zone where Catholics were being violently persecuted, so he took a ship to Portugal and joined his family who were vacationing near Lisbon. A few weeks later, he returned with his family to Spain and immediately joined the Nationalist army. For about a year, he served as an enlisted man, first in Extremadura, in the south of Spain, and then on the Toledo front.

During the first year of the Civil War, Muzquiz had no news of Escrivá. Thousands of priests had been slaughtered in the early months of the conflict for no other reason than that they were priests. Since Escrivá was widely known for his fervor and his activities, Muzquiz assumed that he was among the victims, and that Opus Dei had died with him. In July 1937, Muzquiz was sent to officer candidate school. There he ran into a member of Opus Dei who told him that Escrivá and other members of the Work had survived and were still in Madrid. Muzquiz was pleasantly surprised, but assumed that it was only a matter of time before they would be killed.

In late 1937, after more than a year of hiding-out in Madrid followed by a harrowing trek through the Pyrenees Mountains, Escrivá and a handful of other members of Opus Dei succeeded in reaching Burgos in the Nationalist-controlled part of Spain. There Escrivá was able to resume his priestly activity. In early 1938 he was able to get a message to him. It was brief, but it changed Muzquiz's attitude toward Opus Dei. Given the odds against a well-known priest's surviving in Madrid, escaping from the Republican-controlled part of Spain, and crossing safely into the Nationalist zone, Muzquiz concluded that Opus Dei must be something "supernatural and desired by God."

Shortly after receiving Escrivá's letter, Muzquiz took advantage of a leave to visit him in Burgos. By this time, he was convinced that sooner or later he would join Opus Dei. He began to avoid serious relationships with women so he wouldn't have to break them off in the future. Escrivá had, however, once told him that it would be good to make a retreat before joining, so he felt he couldn't do anything until he was discharged from the army.

In the following months, whenever Muzquiz got to Burgos, on leave or on official business, he made a point of visiting Escrivá. Escrivá encouraged him to attend Mass as often as possible, to find time for mental prayer, to make good use of his time, and to take an interest in his fellow officers, trying to draw them closer to God not only through his example and his ongoing involvement in Catholic Action but also through friendship and personal conversation.

As the months went by, Escrivá became more convinced that Muzquiz was someone whom God was calling to Opus Dei. Bit by bit, he explained to him the details of Opus Dei's spirit of sanctification and apostolate in daily work and told him about what he and the other members of Opus Dei were trying to carry out. Muzquiz drank in Escrivá's explanations of Opus Dei, but in characteristic fashion said very little. As Escrivá commented to one of the early members, "Jose Luis has a great deal of affection for us, but he doesn't say a thing."

~ 3.

JOINING OPUS DEI

THE SPANISH CIVIL WAR ENDED in the spring of 1939, but it was some time before Muzquiz was demobilized. He returned to Madrid at the end of the summer with the sense that he should make a retreat and determine whether God was calling him to join Opus Dei. He put off doing so for fear that he might end up making resolutions he could not fulfill.

On the feast of Christ the King at the end of October 1939, his plans for the day fell through and he decided to drop by the student residence on Jenner Street which the members of Opus Dei had recently opened. Escrivá gave a meditation on Christ the King.[3] He contrasted Christ's kingdom with the earthly political

---

3. Escrivá's "meditations" usually lasted half an hour. He would read a few short passages of the Gospel and comment on them in an intimate personal way, talking out loud with Christ present in the Blessed Sacrament about his life and about the consequences of the Gospel passages he had read for himself and his listeners. In the meditations, Escrivá was not delivering a sermon as an exercise in rhetoric but voicing his own personal conversation with Christ, his personal prayer, as a way of helping the listeners to pray. After his ordination, Muzquiz, like other priests of Opus Dei, adopted this form of preaching. For further information on Escrivá's "meditations," see John F. Coverdale, *Uncommon Faith: The Early Years of Opus Dei (1928-1943)*, pp. 139–142.

dreams that excited many young Spaniards in the months following the end of the civil war. He stressed that the kingdom of Christ, which would have no end, is much greater than any merely human kingdom. "[F]or Christ to reign in the world," he continued, "he has to reign first in your heart. Does he really reign there? Is your heart really for Jesus Christ?" These questions deeply affected Muzquiz and opened up for him new prospects of love and dedication to God. He left the meditation convinced that God was indeed calling him to Opus Dei.

A few weeks later, Escrivá explained to him that in the future there would be other priests of Opus Dei and talked with him about the expansion of the Work throughout the world, encouraging him to study foreign languages. Up to that point, Muzquiz had conceived of Opus Dei exclusively as a group of young laymen around Escrivá. Knowing that there would be priests of Opus Dei helped Muzquiz understand the importance of what Escrivá was doing and how it could become a permanent feature in the life of the Church.

Toward the end of 1939, Muzquiz attended for the first time a Mass celebrated by Escrivá. Although there was nothing unusual about the way in which Escrivá said Mass, Muzquiz came away impressed with his faith and devotion. Around this time he told Escrivá that he would like to make a three- or four-day retreat "to orient his life." Escrivá agreed that it would be a good idea, but didn't press the matter. "Fine," he responded, "we'll have one soon."

On Sunday, January 21, 1940, Muzquiz went to the student residence on Jenner Street to attend a day of recollection, a one-day retreat that Escrivá organized every month. At the time, members of Opus Dei had begun to make weekend trips to Valladolid where they organized formational activities for students in which they explained to them Opus Dei's spirit and the need to have an interior life of prayer and sacrifice, to offer their studies, to live fraternity, etc. In one of the meditations of the day of recollection, Escrivá commented on the passage from the fifth chapter of St. Luke's Gospel, which narrates the first miraculous catch of fish. He took out of his pocket a letter he had received from one of the students who had attended the activities in Valladolid. "I have here a letter from Valladolid," he said. "They are calling us, just as the apostles called those in the other boat."

Muzquiz felt moved by the Holy Spirit to tell Escrivá, whom he and the members of the Work called "the Father," that he was ready to help bring in the catch. "I stayed a few minutes in the oratory. When I came out I saw the Father sitting on a sofa in the hall. He didn't say anything. He seemed to be recollected in prayer, doubtless praying for me, for my vocation. I sat down next to him and told him that I wanted to join the Work. It was all very simple. He responded, 'This is the work of the Holy Spirit.' When I said I would like to talk with him at greater length, he said with great peace and serenity, full of confidence in Our Lord, 'Fine. We'll talk another day.' He gave me a few typewritten pages to read about the supernatural spirit of the Work."

Those pages helped deepen a conviction Muzquiz had arrived at several years earlier: Opus Dei was not merely a well thought out human invention but something positively inspired and willed by God as an instrument at the service of the Church. As Escrivá put it, it had been "born and has developed fulfilling to the letter everything required so that it can be called without boasting the Work of God."

Muzquiz felt certain that he was personally called by God to dedicate his life to Him and His Church in Opus Dei. He was convinced that the members of Opus Dei were, as Escrivá said, "not just men who have joined other men to do a good thing. That is much but it is little. We are fulfilling an imperative command of Christ." This conviction would inform and shape the rest of his life. From the moment he joined Opus Dei, his overriding goal was to incorporate its spirit into his own life and to contribute to spreading its apostolate as the specific way in which God wanted him to serve the Church. Escrivá's prediction was fulfilled in him: "The conviction of the supernatural character of the Work will make you happy sacrificing yourself for its accomplishment."

As seen from the outside, Muzquiz's decision to respond to God's call to serve Him and the Church in Opus Dei did not change the main lines of his life. He continued working as an engineer at the Compañía del Norte, a state-owned railroad where he had just found a job. He stopped going to dances, but he moved in the same social circles, played the same sports, and enjoyed the same recreational activities as before. Inwardly, however, his decision to respond to God's call had a profound, life-changing effect. His daily round of activities took on an entirely new meaning as a way of serving God and the Church. He now saw them as a path to holiness and a means of helping others come closer to God. He continued to pursue many of the goals he had previously set for his life, including professional success, but those aims were subsumed in a larger aspiration. The goal of his life was now to live well, moment by moment, his vocation to Opus Dei. That involved living the virtues and seeking holiness in and through his work and other activities, and spreading to relatives, friends, colleagues, and others the message that they were personally called to holiness in their ordinary, everyday lives.

Following his decision to join Opus Dei, Escrivá explained to him in greater detail the spirit of Opus Dei and what he called "the plan of life" or the "norms": a flexible set of practices of spiritual life designed to help people discover through their daily work and other activities "something holy, something divine, hidden in the most ordinary situations" of work and family life.

Having attended the classes given by Escrivá since early 1936, Muzquiz had learned and put into practice many aspects of the spirit of Opus Dei and concretely the norms. He habitually attended daily Mass, spent some time each day praying before the Blessed Sacrament, and attempted to maintain a lively awareness of God's presence while he worked. Now, however, these things took on new meaning as part of what God was asking of him.

In their conversations, Escrivá strove to help him develop a solid faith, great love of God, and practical confidence in God. At the same time, he taught him small, practical ways of living the virtues day by day. He suggested, for instance, practicing fraternity with the other members of the Work by praying every day the prayer called the *Memorare* for the one who most needed Mary's help. He helped him to see punctuality to meals and other appointments both as a sacrifice that could be offered to God and as a way of living courtesy and demonstrating respect and affection.

In addition to teaching Muzquiz himself, Escrivá asked Alvaro Del Portillo, another civil engineer who had joined Opus Dei in 1935, to give classes on the spirit of Opus Dei to Muzquiz and another recent member, Fernando Valenciano, an engineering student. At Escrivá's suggestion, Muzquiz also sought spiritual direction from Del Portillo. Once a week they got together briefly to talk about Muzquiz's personal spiritual life and his efforts to bring his colleagues, friends, and relatives closer to God. Muzquiz was impressed with the importance Escrivá attributed to his formation, manifested in his willingness to spend time personally and to ask Del Portillo to take time out of a busy schedule to give classes and personal advice on a regular basis to just a couple of people.

Muzquiz worked hard at making his own and following up on the things he learned in his conversations with Escrivá and Del Portillo, in the classes he received from Del Portillo, in meditations and days of recollection, and during a study week organized in the spring of 1940 to give recent vocations to the Work a deeper understanding of its spirit and a more thorough knowledge of how to put it into practice in their daily lives. Thanks to the formation he received, his personal efforts, and the abundant graces God gave him, he soon was living a life of intense prayer and union with God.

HIS DAY BEGAN WITH A MORNING OFFERING which acquired special meaning from his conviction that God had called him with a vocational calling to serve him and the Church in and through his work. As he showered and dressed, he tried to prepare for Mass by praying spiritual communions and saying other aspirations and brief prayers. He dedicated the half hour before Mass to personal prayer before the Blessed Sacrament. That prayer consisted not in reciting fixed formulas but in talking with God.

Muzquiz learned from Escrivá to make Mass the "center and root" of his interior life. Both as a layman and later as a priest, Mass and Communion were for him the most important events of the day, not to be missed even when, because of travel or other circumstances, getting to Mass and Communion meant rising at an early hour, or maintaining for many hours the Eucharistic fast, which at that time required not eating or drinking anything from midnight until after one received Communion. At Mass, in union with Christ's sacrifice, Muzquiz offered to God his work and other activities which took on greater value precisely by being associated with the Mass.

Before leaving for work in the morning, he usually spent a few minutes reading one of the books of the New Testament, trying not simply to read for information, but to participate in the events described as if he had been present. Often he found in the passage he read a phrase to repeat as an aspiration during the day or a thought that he came back to later in his mental prayer. In addition to daily reading of the New Testament, Muzquiz found ten to fifteen minutes each day to read the Old Testament or a book of spirituality, whether classics like St. Theresa of Avila's autobiography or more recent books. At Escrivá's suggestion, he focused especially on books that dealt with the life of spiritual childhood, like *Story of a Soul* by St. Thérèse of Lisieux.

On his way to and from work, Muzquiz liked to glance at the pictures and statues of Our Lady that could be seen on many buildings and at street corners in Madrid, taking advantage of the occasion to pray to her. He habitually said the Rosary walking to and from work. Sometimes he tried to concentrate on the words of the Hail Mary. Other times he focused on the intentions for which he offered each decade. Most times, however, he tried to follow Escrivá's advice on contemplating the mysteries by entering each of the scenes:

> *The beginning of the way*, at the end of which you will find yourself completely carried away with love for Jesus, is a confident love for Mary.

> —Do you want to love Our Lady?—Well, get to know her. How?—By praying her Rosary *well.*

> [. . .] Before each decade we are told the mystery to be *contemplated.*

> —Have you . . . ever *contemplated* these mysteries?

> *Become little.* Come with me and—this is the essence of what I have to confide—we will live the life of Jesus, Mary, and Joseph.

> Each day we will render them a new service. We will hear their family conversations. We will see the Messiah grow up. We will admire His thirty years of hidden life . . . We will be present at His Passion and Death . . . We will be awed by the Glory of His Resurrection . . . In a word: we will contemplate, carried away with Love (the only real love is Love), each and every moment of the life of Christ Jesus.

At noon, Muzquiz interrupted his work for a moment to pray the *Angelus,* to review how he had done during the morning on the particular point of interior struggle he was concentrating on at the time, and to make a plan for the rest of the day with regard to that point. Often the focus of his particular examination of conscience was on his effort to sanctify his work and to make it a means of sanctification for himself and others. Sometimes this involved working more carefully, making better use of his time, or having a greater spirit of service and collegiality. Other times it involved trying to remember to offer his work for particular intentions including the Pope, the Bishop of Madrid, Escrivá, other members of Opus Dei, friends and colleagues, and peace in the world. He tried to maintain his awareness of God's presence by saying aspirations and other short prayers throughout the day and by invoking the protection of his own guardian angel and of the guardian angels of people he met.

After work, he dedicated another half hour to mental prayer, usually before the Blessed Sacrament in the oratory of the Opus Dei center or in a church. In the evening before going to bed he stopped in the oratory of the center for a few minutes to examine his conscience and make an act of contrition and a resolution for the next day.

MUZQUIZ'S HUMAN AND SUPERNATURAL MATURITY and the sincerity and generosity of his response to God's call led Escrivá to rely heavily on him and to entrust him promptly with many responsibilities. Until 1940, Escrivá, who was still the only priest of Opus Dei, not only preached numerous retreats and days of recollection but personally gave all the classes of doctrinal and spiritual formation. By 1940, however, the number of members of Opus Dei and the number of people attending the circles and other apostolic activities had grown to the point that he was swamped. In February 1940, he decided to turn over the circles to others. Although Muzquiz had only recently joined the Work, he was one of the people to whom Escrivá entrusted this task.

When the first member of Opus Dei, Isidoro Zorzano, fell ill with Hodgkin's disease and had to be hospitalized, Escrivá asked Muzquiz to arrange for him to be accompanied twenty-four hours a day by members of the Work. Muzquiz took this responsibility very seriously. For months on end some member of the Work was with Isidoro day and night. On July 15, 1943, however, a mix-up occurred and for a brief period Isidoro was left alone. He died during that interval, accompanied only by the nuns who ran the clinic. Muzquiz took full personal responsibility for the breakdown of the system he had established. He was deeply upset that a brother of his in Opus Dei should have died without the company of any member of the Work. Perhaps for this reason, when Isidoro's cause of canonization was opened some years later, Escrivá gave Muzquiz responsibility for the cause. Throughout his life Muzquiz often prayed to Isidoro and talked about him.

Opus Dei was beginning to put down roots outside Madrid. At the time, most people had at least a half a day of work or classes on Saturdays, so the members of the Work had only Sundays to contact people outside the capital. They would leave Madrid Saturday evening and spend the night sitting up on the hard seats of a jolting overnight train to Valladolid, Zaragoza, or Barcelona. On arrival, they would pray to the guardian angel of the city and to the guardian angels of the people they would meet during the day. They would try to reach students whose names had been given to them by friends in Madrid, but if that failed they would head out to see whom they could meet on the street where students could be found taking a Sunday *paseo*. After spending the day meeting and talking to young people and giving circles, they would spend another sleepless night on the train, arriving back in Madrid just in time to go to Mass and resume their work or studies.

On several occasions when Escrivá accompanied them on these trips, he pointed out to them in the meditation that they were imitating the example of the first Christians, who traveled from place to place to spread the Gospel and to encourage and support those who had recently decided to follow Christ. This, he told them, was their concrete way of serving the Church, which he encouraged them to love with all their heart: "What joy to be able to say with all the fervor of my soul: I love my Mother, the holy Church." Thanks to these trips, a number of people joined Opus Dei. Although Muzquiz's own vocation was recent, Escrivá entrusted to him the formation of some of the people who had recently discovered their calling to the Work.

MUZQUIZ'S PROFESSIONAL COMPETENCE, CALM, poise, good humor, and piety were an inspiration both to other young members of Opus Dei and to students who were thinking about their possible call to Opus Dei. Laureano López Rodó, a future Commissioner of Economic Development and Minister of Foreign Affairs, but at the time a law student, was struck by Muzquiz's smiling good humor when they met in Barcelona in 1940.

During a conversation with Escrivá in Madrid a short time later, López Rodó began to think about dedicating himself fully to God in the midst of the world as a member of Opus Dei. At first he was enthused with the prospect, but as the hours wore on he began to think that such a vocation was "marvelous but impossible." That same evening Muzquiz accompanied him to the station to catch the night train back to Barcelona. "Seeing him so serene and smiling," López Rodó recalls, "I immediately reached a conclusion: the life of total dedication is possible, since Jose Luis Muzquiz lives it. I immediately became calm, and slept solidly the whole night despite the fact that I was sitting up in a second-class car."

People who accompanied Muzquiz on weekend trips to outlying cities were impressed with how well he used his time. Teodoro Ruiz, a student from Valladolid who joined Opus Dei in the spring of 1940, recalls a trip to Barcelona: "I was impressed with his extraordinary ability to make use of his time. The trip was long and uncomfortable, but he spent the whole time reading or writing, undisturbed by the jolting of the train. The trip took longer than expected. Because of flooding, the train had to stop in the middle of the country. He just continued working. He only stopped to go briefly to a nearby farmhouse to buy something to eat. He managed to find a little bread and a can of sardines. That is all we had to eat during the many hours we spent there blocked by the floods, but Jose Luis never lost his good humor."

MUZQUIZ'S MEMBERSHIP IN OPUS DEI soon made him an object of criticism and controversy. In the years following the Spanish Civil War, Opus Dei encountered opposition from some members of the government-sponsored political party, the Falange, who resented Opus Dei's insistence on the freedom of Catholics to make their own political choices without being involved in the Falange or its associated organizations. A much more important flood of criticism and even persecution came from some members of religious orders. Their animosity toward Opus Dei may have been motivated by a sincere belief that the only way to pursue sanctity seriously was to separate oneself from the world by joining an order. In some cases they may also have feared that young men and women who might otherwise have thought of joining their own order would prefer to serve God in the world as members of Opus Dei.

Muzquiz, who held national office in Catholic Action and who continued to be active in the Jesuit-sponsored Sodality of Our Lady, soon found himself forced to withdraw from those organizations by criticism of his membership in Opus Dei and by accusations that he was trying to infiltrate them to entice their members to switch their loyalties to Opus Dei. Far more painful to Muzquiz was the fact that members of a religious order, including an uncle of his, repeatedly visited his family to warn his parents that he was putting his soul in danger by joining Opus Dei. Muzquiz's father was not much disturbed by the warnings and quickly came to understand and support his son's vocation. His mother, however, was deeply upset and accepted and appreciated his vocation only years later.

Muzquiz bore this suffering peacefully and patiently. Neither at the time nor later did he criticize the people responsible.

Years later, his sister mentioned to him that their family had not been named in a biography of the founder of Opus Dei which spoke of the efforts to turn the families of early members against Opus Dei. Muzquiz limited himself to responding: "That's good. Our family was one of the ones they most upset, but the person who visited them most often eventually asked the Father's pardon."

During his trips to Barcelona, where the persecution was particularly vicious, Muzquiz passed on to the few young men who had joined Opus Dei Escrivá's prescription for dealing with the situation: "Be quiet, pardon, smile." Although his conversation and the talks he gave them were simple and unadorned, his own cheerful serenity was an important source of peace for them in the midst of a tense and painful environment. He had not been in Opus Dei much longer than they had, but they saw him as an older brother on whom they could rely. Thanks in part to his support, the members of the Work in Barcelona, most of them still college students who had belonged to Opus Dei for only a short time, were able to see the persecution they endured as something that God wanted to send them. "They don't even talk about it," Muzquiz told Escrivá.

AMONG THE THINGS ABOUT MUZQUIZ THAT STRUCK even other members of the Work was how determined he was to serve God and the Church by carrying out Opus Dei. In a retreat preached by Escrivá in July 1941, Muzquiz took notes of Escrivá's insistence on the need for complete dedication: "We can respond or not to the call. But once we respond, we have to follow the Way just as God has laid it out." "Be a saint or leave. We must deal with Jesus Christ. We must cut whatever gets in the way. Cutting the chain will be easy. But we have to cut the threads of the spider web [that hold us back]. Anything else is to say 'I don't want to.' It is to not really want. . . . Better than half-way measures is to have the sincerity to tell Our Lord here in the tabernacle: 'Look, here you have a child of yours who tells you no.'"

From the beginning of his life as a member of Opus Dei, Muzquiz struggled hard to respond wholeheartedly to God's call. His work as a railroad engineer at a time when Spain was attempting to rebuild the railroads destroyed or damaged during the Civil War was extremely demanding. In addition he spent several hours each day attending Mass, meditating, and living the rest of the norms of piety he had learned from Escrivá. Nonetheless he found a great deal of time for people, both for his friends and for the other members of Opus Dei. One of them recalls: "Every minute of the day was a service to God and to his brothers. Either he was praying or carrying out tasks entrusted to him by our Father,[4] or speaking with someone, encouraging them and helping them live with more dedication to God and interior life. I don't recall his reserving any time for listening to music or other forms of relaxation. I am convinced that Jose Luis spent his time talking with God or talking about God with others. He clearly was very demanding on himself and austere. He didn't seem to need anything for himself, and he didn't complain about the discomforts of frequent trips on the trains of the time. After a night or two nights on the train without sleeping, he continued working all-out. Being with him was a lesson in how to be quietly mortified and self-sacrificing."

Muzquiz understood his vocation to Opus Dei as a call to bring many others closer to God and to help some of them to discover that God wanted them to serve Him and the Church in Opus Dei. Because the apostolate of Opus Dei is primarily carried out one-on-one by word and example in the give-and-take of daily life, Muzquiz was anxious to increase the circle of his

---

4. From the beginning of Opus Dei, the members addressed Escrivá as "Father," and spoke about him among themselves as "the Father." In the statutes of Opus Dei, Escrivá established that his successors as head of Opus Dei should be addressed as "Father." Using the term "the Father" to refer to both Escrivá and the current head of Opus Dei would obviously lead to confusion. To avoid that, when Del Portillo succeeded Escrivá he suggested that they refer to Escrivá as "our Father," and to him and his successors as "the Father." Thus the phrase "our Father" in this and other quotes means Escrivá.

friends and acquaintances. He reached out especially to other engineers at work and in meetings with professional colleagues, and tried to encourage those with whom he had become friends to take their Christian vocation more seriously.

He also tried to get to know people outside the immediate circles in which he moved. In the early 1940s he frequently attended Sunday morning lectures on cultural topics at the British Institute where he met people he would not have encountered elsewhere. In Franco's Spain during the early years of World War II, going to the British Institute required some courage. Spain was not officially allied with the Axis, but Germany and Italy had supported Franco during the Civil War and both official and public opinion were strongly pro-German and anti-British.

As Muzquiz approached the end of his second year as a member of Opus Dei, he exhibited a remarkable degree of maturity in converting his daily life as a young engineer deeply involved in helping his country recover from the Civil War into a path that brought closer to God both him and the people with whom he was in touch. He was well on his way to making a reality in his own life Escrivá's ideal of being a man of prayer and an apostle while remaining immersed in his profession and in the life of his country.

~⌒ 4.

A PRIEST OF OPUS DEI

AT THE END OF ITS FIRST DECADE OF EXISTENCE, Opus Dei appeared to be a group of young lay men and women gathered around a diocesan priest. From the beginning, Escrivá had conceived of it as comprised of both priests and laity, but for the moment he was the only priest. He was convinced that the future priests would have to be drawn from among the lay members, but neither his own study of canon law nor his consultations with experts had revealed any viable path for ordaining priests who would serve the Church by dedicating themselves primarily to providing pastoral attention to the members of Opus Dei and to collaborating in its apostolic activities.

The problem, in fact, was not an easy one. Opus Dei had recently been approved by the Bishop of Madrid as a pious union, but that gave it no right to have priests of its own.[5] More important, there did not appear to be any legal category into

---

5. Escrivá himself was a diocesan priest of the diocese of Madrid. He had been ordained for the diocese of Zaragoza and in 1927 had been granted permission to move to Madrid to obtain a doctorate in civil law. In 1934 he was transferred to the diocese of Madrid.

which Opus Dei could fit that would allow it to have priests ordained. Under church law, in general a man could be called to the priesthood only by the bishop of a diocese or the head of a religious order or of a group similar to a religious order. In addition, a priest had to be "incardinated," i.e., form part of a particular diocese or religious order or similar institution. Opus Dei was not a diocese. It was not and could not become a religious order or anything similar to a religious order because its members were not religious but lay men and women and its priests would be secular priests. They were called by God to sanctify themselves in and through their work and other activities in the world, not to leave the world as the members of religious orders do.

Although Escrivá still had not found any solution to this knotty problem, sometime in late 1941 or early 1942 he asked Muzquiz if he would like to be ordained as a priest of Opus Dei. In Escrivá's mind, and in the mind of the members of the Work, becoming a priest did not represent a new vocation different from that they had as members of Opus Dei. It did not even represent a culmination to which the lay members should aspire. Rather it was simply another way of serving God as a member of Opus Dei. This may explains the striking brevity and simplicity of the conversation in which Escrivá posed the question of ordination. As Muzquiz recalls it, he simply asked him, "My son, would you like to be a priest?" When he said, "Yes, Father, I'd be delighted," he responded, "Then talk with Alvaro about studies."

Although Muzquiz was aware that Escrivá still had not found any way in which Opus Dei could have priests ordained, he had complete faith that he would find one and began studying for the priesthood as if there were no problem. Preparing for ordination involved a formidable amount of work. In addition to the philosophical and theological studies the Church required of all priests, Escrivá wanted the priests of Opus Dei to have a civil doctorate. At the time no university in Spain offered a doctorate in engineering, so Muzquiz would have to earn a doctorate in some other subject.

Escrivá's original plans called for ordaining a first group made up of Alvaro Del Portillo and José María Hernández de Garnica, both engineers. Muzquiz would form part of a second group comprising himself and José Orlandis, a lawyer who later became a distinguished historian. During the summer of 1942 Muzquiz and Orlandis studied privately and passed their philosophy exams in the Madrid seminary. In the fall, when Orlandis moved to Rome to study canon law, Escrivá told Muzquiz that he could either do extra studying to catch up with Del Portillo and Hernández de Garnica, or wait and join the next group. In light of Opus Dei's urgent need for priests to take care of its rapidly growing apostolates, Muzquiz chose to join the first group.

Escrivá assembled a distinguished faculty of theology professors to teach the three first priests of Opus Dei. Among them were a future cardinal and two future bishops, two professors of the Angelicum University in Rome, and a professor of the Pontifical Biblical Institute in Jerusalem. The Angelicum and Biblical Institute professors had been caught in Spain by the outbreak of World War II and were unable to return to their home institutions.

Escrivá personally took charge of the spiritual, pastoral, and apostolic formation of the three. Building on Christ's statement that the "Son of Man did not come to be served but to serve," he stressed that the role of priests in Opus Dei is to serve, not to give orders. He advised them to "Be priests first of all. And then, priests. And always and in everything, *only priests*. Speak only about God. When a penitent wants you, drop whatever you are doing and take care of him." "The priests of Opus Dei," he told them, "are not the best members or the most learned. They are those whom God wants." "Being a priest," he added, "is simply a necessary service, another way of serving."

On the other hand, Escrivá stressed that because of the role he plays a priest is "another Christ, Christ himself." Given this dignity, any imperfection in a priest is important. Infidelity on the part of a priest is extraordinarily displeasing to God because of the grandeur of the priestly ministry. But they should be full of confidence, he said, because the Lord had chosen them and he would lead them to a happy outcome in their own sanctification and in their apostolate. To fulfill their mission of service, they would need to have a solid interior life of prayer and sacrifice. Escrivá insisted: "You have to carry on a continual conversation with God. When something goes wrong, you have to see it from God's perspective. When you are humiliated, you have to offer it to God."

From time to time the three future priests, each of whom had many professional and apostolic responsibilities in Madrid, spent a few days outside the city studying for exams. On February 15, 1943, Escrivá went to see them in El Escorial, a small town about thirty miles northwest of Madrid. He told Alvaro Del Portillo that the previous morning, while celebrating Mass, he had seen the solution to the problem of ordaining priests for Opus Dei. It would be called the Priestly Society of the Holy Cross. Its members would be the priests of Opus Dei and some lay members of the Work who were preparing for ordination. Much still remained to be done to make this a reality, but a path had been identified and the goal was now in sight. Escrivá immediately set to work to obtain the necessary approvals. The Holy See gave its *nihil obstat* in October 1943, and the Bishop of Madrid canonically erected the Priestly Society of the Holy Cross and Opus Dei on December 8, 1943.

To have more time for his studies, Muzquiz requested a leave of absence from the railroad in May 1943. He continued working as a consulting structural engineer in an office he had established in 1941, and in fall 1943 took on new responsibilities as director of one of Opus Dei's centers in Madrid and as a member of

Opus Dei's governing body, the General Council. Even without working for the railroad, his days were still packed.

While carrying out his ecclesiastical studies, Muzquiz also studied history at the University of Valencia, he finished his licenciate degree, roughly equivalent to an American Master's degree. Given the many things he had to do, one might have expected him to chose a topic for his doctoral dissertation that could be completed using readily available printed sources. Instead he decided to undertake archival work both in Madrid and Seville. Professor Ponz, who spent a week or ten days with him in a small house in the country near Avila studying and writing, paints a portrait of Muzquiz seated on the ground in the open air surrounded by piles of notes held down with pebbles while writing furiously from morning to night with barely a break except for meals and to pray. Muzquiz presented his Ph.D. dissertation in history on May 12, 1944. It won the University of Madrid's equivalent of summa cum laude and was published shortly after its completion.

MUZQUIZ, DEL PORTILLO, and Hernández de Garnica were ordained on June 25, 1944, by the Bishop of Madrid, Leopoldo Eijo y Garay, in his chapel. A large congregation overflowed the chapel. In addition to members of Opus Dei, family members, friends, and professional colleagues, there were priests from the offices of the archbishop and of the Papal Nuncio as well as other diocesan priests and members of many religious orders.

That afternoon Escrivá gave a meditation in Opus Dei's center on Lagasca Street in Madrid. So many members of the Work from all over the country were there that they spilled out of the oratory into the hall. As Muzquiz along with the other two recently ordained priests listened from outside the oratory, Escrivá insisted on the need for personal and collective humility and for a deep interior life of prayer and sacrifice: "When the youngest of you are going gray—or sporting splendid bald spots—and I, by the law of nature, have long since departed, others are going to ask you: 'What did the Father say on the day of the ordination of the first three?' And you will answer them: 'He said prayer, prayer, prayer.'"

Father Joseph Muzquiz celebrated his first solemn Mass on June 29, 1944, in the church of the Monastery of the Incarnation. In the pews were many former classmates from the School of Engineering and employees of the railroad where he had worked. Following the custom of the time, at the end of the Mass people came up to kiss Father Joseph's newly consecrated hands. When Escrivá approached, the normally self-contained Muzquiz was so moved that he was unable to say anything to him.

AT A TIME WHEN MOST secular priests came from modest country or small-town families and when few priests had studied outside the seminary, the news of the ordination of three upper-middle-class graduates of the most prestigious professional school in Spain was widely reported in the press. The news had wide impact and changed lives. Dorita Calvo, a young woman who was working in a government office, recalls, "I was caught up in a frivolous world, and my life was empty. Practically my only goal was to have a good time and little more." The article made her think: "Those men, who are so young and so handsome, have given up everything for God. And me, what am I doing?" Together with a group of friends, she organized a retreat and invited a professor in the seminary of Madrid to preach it. "I came out of that retreat changed, ready to give God whatever he asked me for, my entire life."

Calvo had not focused on the fact that the three young priests whose example had so moved her belonged to Opus Dei, about which she knew nothing. She assumed that dedicating herself to God necessarily meant becoming a nun, but she couldn't quite believe that God was asking that of her. "With all the work it took to pass the exam and get the job I have, how can I renounce it all now all at once? God would have made me see sooner if that was what he wanted." Eventually a priest suggested that she get in contact with Opus Dei.

As she was waiting for the streetcar one day to go to a center of Opus Dei, she noticed Father Joseph waiting for the streetcar. Although he looked somehow familiar, she could not place him. "I was impressed by his dignity. His face was that of a person who is very close to God, without being sanctimonious. He wore a clean new cassock. His bearing was elegant and there was something spiritual about him that I couldn't define." They both got off the streetcar at the same stop, and moments later Calvo saw Muzquiz ring the doorbell of the center she was going to. "I was so taken with his dignity and I felt such respect for him that . . . I waited until he had gone in before I rang the bell."

That same afternoon Calvo spoke at length with Muzquiz. "I told him about my inner problem—God's call—and my search for the right place to give myself to God. I also said that I liked Opus Dei, but that from what I had seen it didn't involve the change of life God was asking of me. I had seen that the house was attractive and that the members of the Work were well dressed, so I supposed they lived a comfortable life, whereas God was asking me for everything." Father Joseph clarified that belonging to Opus Dei involved total self-giving. He went into detail to show her that the lives of the young women in the center involved great sacrifice, and urged her not to be deceived by appearances. Muzquiz stressed that the call to Opus Dei was a vocation to sanctity, and that sanctity can only be achieved with total self-giving. A short time later, Calvo joined Opus Dei.

FATHER JOSEPH PREACHED A RETREAT for the first time in August 1944 in Valencia. He shared the preaching with Hernández de Garnica. In a letter to Escrivá written during the retreat he reported that "we find it hard to shout and move our hands, but let's see if somehow we manage."

Shortly after Father Joseph's ordination, Escrivá asked him to provide pastoral care for Opus Dei's incipient activities in southern Spain. Following the Civil War, Opus Dei had first expanded into cities north and east of Madrid (Valladolid, Zaragoza, Barcelona, and Valencia), and only in 1943 did it begin activities in the South. That fall a few young students who had recently joined the Work began studying at the University of Seville where another member, Vicente Rodríguez Casado, was professor of history. Rodríguez Casado happened also to be the director of Casa Seras, a small residence recently established for students and researchers by the School of Spanish-American studies. The residence was far from full, so the members of Opus Dei were able to live there, although it had no connection with Opus Dei.

In December 1943, Muzquiz accompanied Escrivá and Del Portillo on a trip to Seville. They visited the members of the Work, and, in addition, Muzquiz and Del Portillo were able to do some research in the Archive of the Indies for their doctoral theses in history.

Muzquiz took careful note of the instructions Escriva gave him before he began his own apostolic trips to the South. The goal of the trips, Escrivá told him, should be to contribute to the formation of the other members of the Work, to keep him informed and to direct and promote their apostolic activities. To do this, Escrivá stressed, he should rely on supernatural means: prayer (considering in his mental prayer the goals of the trip, the characteristics of the persons he would be seeing, the problems, and the reports he needed to make), mortification (above all living order and making good use of time), and interior life (cultivating the sense of God's presence, being cheerful and united with one another).

Father Joseph spent the first two weeks of December 1944 in the South, accompanied by López Rodó. They went by train to Granada where they met a number of people. Both Muzquiz and López Rodó talked individually with the students they met about the ideal of living a deeply Christian life in the midst of the world, and encouraged them to introduce other students to them. Father Joseph heard confessions and gave a meditation. They also took advantage of their stay in the city to search for a house in which to establish a residence for university students, but were unable to find anything suitable. From Granada they went by bus to Malaga where a priest introduced them to a number of people. There too they met and talked with students and searched in vain for a house that could serve as a center of Opus Dei.

Finally they took a train from Malaga to Seville. The train was so crowded that they had to stand the entire way, but Muzquiz managed to write a letter to Escrivá informing him about what they had done so far. López Rodo, who found that the movement of the train and the jostling of the other passengers made it impossible to write, recalls: "It was an example of how to use time well and of his desire to have the Father receive as soon as possible a letter with news of our first 'discoveries' in those cities of Andalucía."

During his stay in Seville, Father Joseph preached a retreat in the oratory of Casa Seras for members of the Work and their friends. Although not a gifted orator, he was an effective preacher. His style was simple, going straight to the point without long introductions or embellishments. A university professor commented: "I've never heard anyone preach in such a simple way, without rhetoric and with so little concern for style, and yet so penetratingly and convincingly."

During the retreat, Muzquiz found time to meet individually with each of the participants for confession and personal spiritual direction. His style in spiritual direction was similar to his preaching, simple but clear and effective. According to a priest who knew him well, "He listened and asked questions amiably. He often made use of passages of Scripture or of the teaching and example of the Father, illustrated with short but clear examples, frequently drawn from the world of engineering. He suggested concrete goals and resolutions. He combined prudent understanding for the weakness of others with making demands." Shortly after the retreat, a student, Joaquín Rueda, joined Opus Dei and sometime later several others followed in his footsteps.

Beginning with this first one, trips to the South became part of Muzquiz's regular routine. He would take the uncomfortable overnight train from Madrid to Seville, shave in the tiny and none-too-clean bathroom of the train, and arrive at the center smiling and ready to work despite having gotten little sleep. In late March and early April 1945 Muzquiz traveled with Escrivá throughout Andalucía. In addition to pastoral activities, they continued to search in Seville and Granada for buildings suitable for a residence. In Seville they found an elegant well-located three-story house with a large interior patio with a fountain. Muzquiz took measurements and drew plans of the building which soon became the University Residence del Arenal, later renamed Guadaira. In Granada they found a building on the outskirts of the city where the Albayzín University Residence would open its doors in the fall of 1945.

EARLY IN 1945, MUZQUIZ ADDED TO HIS DUTIES by accepting an appointment as professor of religion and ethics at the School of Engineering of Roads, Canals, and Ports. That summer, together with Alvaro Del Portillo and José María Hernández Garnica, he taught classes, celebrated Mass, and gave spiritual direction to the participants in the first full-scale course of formation for women members of the Work. It was conducted in a newly acquired center called Los Rosales, located in the small town of Villaviciosa de Odón a little more than ten miles southwest of Madrid.

A number of the young women who attended this course would later begin the apostolate of Opus Dei with women in other countries—Italy, England, the United States, Mexico, Guatemala, Chile, Colombia, and Venezuela. One of the participants commented years later that seeing how Muzquiz lived the spirit of Opus Dei "affected me deeply and helped me to understand the spirit of the Work better and better. He transmitted it to us with his words, but especially with his example."

During the summer Father Joseph also visited the college-age members of the Work who were required to spend most of the summer at a military training camp located near Ronda, a small town to the west of Málaga in the heart of Andalucía. They were impressed by his good humor as he sat chatting with them in the shade of a tree, dripping with sweat in the 100-degree heat after walking from Ronda under the blazing sun in full clerical garb and giving them a meditation.

Forty years later one of them, José Luis González-Simancas, still recalled with gratitude the fortitude combined with affection with which Muzquiz corrected him when he told him privately about something that had happened the previous day. During a class, another student who knew he belonged to Opus Dei had leaned over and whispered "Opus Dei, Opus Diaboli." [Work of God, Work of the Devil]. González-Simancas had glared at him but had not responded. Father Joseph, he recalls, "told me that I had been a coward, and that I had to learn to defend the Work without inferiority complexes. He said that the next day I should look for that student and correct him energetically, demanding that he beg my pardon for what he had said." González-Simancas did so the next morning, and the two ended up friends.

In 1946, Muzquiz also traveled to northwestern Spain and Portugal to help Opus Dei's activities there. The trips were often slow and difficult, marked by long delays. On one occasion it took 24 hours to cover the 375 miles between Madrid and La Coruña, which meant that he did not arrive till 2:00 p.m. That did not keep him from celebrating Mass when he arrived, despite the fact that at the time priests had to abstain from food and water from midnight until after Mass. On another occasion the ramshackle car in which he traveled together with nine other people and their packages had so many flat tires that it didn't reach its destination until three in the morning. The car belonged to a newspaper called *The Night. Urgent News.* Muzquiz commented jokingly to Escrivá, "The news may be urgent, but the car was in no hurry."

In 1946, Opus Dei opened its first center in Portugal in the university town of Coimbra. In October, Muzquiz visited Coimbra. He made several more trips to Portugal during the final months of 1946 and spent Christmas there. He said Mass, preached meditations, heard confessions, gave spiritual direction, and encouraged the members of the Work who were still getting their bearings in a new country and trying to learn the language. Muzquiz himself knew some Portuguese from his family's summer stays there before the Spanish Civil War and from a research trip he had made in 1941, but he was far from fluent. On one occasion when he was attempting to speak Portuguese the person he was speaking with commented that his Spanish sounded like Portuguese.

During the 1947–48 school year, two members of Opus Dei, Florencio Sánchez Bella and Vicente Lombardía, moved to Córdoba where Lombardía had inherited a family pharmaceutical manufacturing business. Initially they lived in ramshackle quarters in the factory. Sánchez Bella recalls that Muzquiz's zeal and good spirit helped them "supernaturalize those circumstances. He helped us grow in the theological virtues, teaching us to have much faith in God, great hope for the future of our work, and a love of God that would manifest itself in fraternity and in a spirit of proselytism. . . . He assured us that God would make up with his grace for what we were unable to do." Things were not as tight as they had been in Granada where they often could not pay the grocery bills, but they had serious problems meeting mortgage payments. Father Joseph taught them to accept these difficulties cheerfully and with love for the spirit of poverty.

Muzquiz visited Rome for the first time in June 1947. Escrivá had gone there a year earlier and in February 1947 had obtained the Holy See's approval of Opus Dei. As soon as

Muzquiz reached the small apartment near St. Peter's Square where Escrivá and the other members of Opus Dei were living, Escrivá pointed out to him with great veneration the windows of the papal apartment which could be seen from the balcony. Escrivá then took him to St. Peter's Basilica to pray the Creed. The Basilica was closed, so they prayed outside. On June 29, the feast of Saints Peter and Paul, Father Joseph celebrated Mass at a side altar in St. Peter's with great emotion.

The next day Muzquiz had an audience with Pope Pius XII. When he told the Holy Father that he belonged to Opus Dei, Pius XII interjected, "I approved it." Several times as Muzquiz told him about some of Opus Dei's activities the Pope exclaimed in Spanish, "¡*Qué lindo!*" [How beautiful!] Thirty years later, Muzquiz still remembered not only the Pope's commentaries but his Argentine accent acquired during his diplomatic service there.

PART II

STARTING OPUS DEI IN THE UNITED STATES

—— 1949–1961 ——

~5.

FIRST STEPS IN
THE UNITED STATES

FROM THE FOUNDATION OF OPUS DEI IN 1928, Escrivá had been
convinced that God wanted it to serve the Church by spreading throughout the world the message that God wants all men
and women to seek sanctity, most of them in the setting of
everyday life. In 1948 he decided that the time had come for
Opus Dei—which had already begun its activities in Italy, Portugal, England, France, and Ireland—to cross the Atlantic.
He was especially anxious to begin in the United States both
because of American influence in the world and because José
María González Barredo, one of the first members of Opus
Dei, had been in the United States for several years doing
research in physics and had painted a glowing picture of the
possibilities there.[6]

---

6. In 1946 Barredo had won a three-year fellowship for post-doctoral work in physics. Escrivá had suggested that he consider looking for a post-doctoral position in
the United States so that he could get to know the country and study firsthand the
possibilities for Opus Dei's apostolate there.

In preparation for beginning Opus Dei in the Americas, Father Pedro Casciaro and two other members of the Work spent six months visiting bishops and university officials and collecting first-hand impressions of the United States, Canada, Mexico, Peru, Chile, and Argentina. In September 1948 Escrivá told Muzquiz that Casciaro would be leaving soon for an as yet to be determined destination in America. "Perhaps in a year or so . . . we'll send you there also." Although Muzquiz was interested in going to the United States, he said nothing so as to leave Escrivá free to send him wherever he thought best.

A few days later Escrivá suggested that Muzquiz might go immediately to the United States: "As you know, Pedro spent quite a bit of time in Mexico and knows the environment. How would it be if instead of starting in one country in America we were to start in two? Pedro could go to Mexico. Would you like to go to the United States?" Muzquiz responded that he would be delighted, and Escrivá told him to look for a few young members of the Work who could accompany him. Sal Ferigle, a physicist who was close to finishing his Ph.D., was the first to volunteer. He was soon joined by José María Viladas ("Joe") and Antonio Martorell ("Tony").

Months would go by before Muzquiz and his companions could complete their arrangements to leave for the U.S. In the meantime, Father Joseph carried on his priestly activities, including his duties with regard to Isidoro Zorzano's cause for beatification and canonization. The cause was formally opened in Madrid on October 11, 1948. A few days later, during a trip they made together to Portugal, Escrivá advised Muzquiz to pray to Isidoro for the apostolate in the United States.

In December Muzquiz and Ferigle attended a retreat preached by Escrivá. Years later, Father Joseph commented on that retreat, "I will always remember how energetically the Father insisted on the need for humility and on the great dangers of pride. To be aware that it is the Lord who does everything, and that we are only instruments, was a good preparation for beginning in a new country."

Escrivá urged Muzquiz not be afraid of making mistakes: "It's better to have to turn back in two things than to fail to do ninety-eight for fear of making a mistake." He stressed the importance of not isolating themselves in a foreign ghetto, of speaking English even among themselves, and of becoming fully American. At the same time, he said, they had to avoid loving their new country so much that they failed to see its defects and therefore failed to try to correct them. Beginning in the United States would not be easy: "You will find hard ground, with thorns and thistles. You will have to put your soul into your apostolic work, as the plow is thrust into dry ground."

Opus Dei was so hard-pressed for money that Escrivá told Muzquiz regretfully that he could only give him his blessing. "But," Father Joseph recalled, "the Father's affection and his love for Our Lady found something more valuable than money for us to take to the United States. He gave us a picture of Our Lady which had been in the center of Opus Dei in Burgos during the Spanish Civil War."

Muzquiz found it impossible to obtain a resident visa, so he opted for traveling with a tourist visa in the hope of later being admitted as a resident. He and Ferigle left Madrid by plane shortly after midnight on February 17, 1949. The plane stopped in Lisbon, the Azores, and Newfoundland before landing in New York in the late afternoon of February 17. At each stop they sent a postcard to Escrivá. On the last leg of the trip, Muzquiz wrote from the plane: "We have been flying for five hours over a small part of America. A few minutes ago we passed over Boston. We picked out Harvard University . . . and prayed to the guardian angel of the university and to the guardian angels of each of the inhabitants. I think we will keep them busy. They must be sort of unemployed. The country is very big . . . and very small. And all of it has to be filled with tabernacles. . . . We are very happy and

45

have great desires to work. From the plane you see immense horizons. What a great harvest!"[7]

Barredo met Muzquiz and Ferigle at the airport. Father Joseph said Mass for the first time in the United States in the Church of St. Paul the Apostle on 59th Street, near Columbus Circle. The three of them went to Boston, where they spoke with some people Barredo had met earlier, among them the author Daniel Sargent, who would later write a biography of Isidoro Zorzano. At St. Benedict's Center, Father Joseph gave a talk about Isidoro which went over well despite his difficulties in English.[8]

Muzquiz and Barredo then traveled to Washington, D.C. where they met with the Apostolic Delegate as well as with some people at the official Spanish-language Catholic news agency who offered to send out information about Zorzano and about Opus Dei. On February 24 they returned to New York where they joined Ferigle, as well as Viladas and Martorell who had just flown in from Spain.

In New York Barredo introduced Ferigle to a twenty-two-year-old acquaintance of his who had studied in Canada although his African father and French mother still lived in France. The young man was working at Friendship House in Harlem. Walking around Central Park, Ferigle explained Opus Dei to the young man. He was enthused with what he heard and later traveled to Chicago, where he decided to join Opus Dei but immediately changed his mind.

---

7. Because Jesus present in the Eucharist is the heart of every Opus Dei center, Escrivá often spoke about a new tabernacle rather than a new center. Muzquiz's phrase about filling the United States with tabernacles expressed his hope that Opus Dei would have many centers in the country.

8. Barredo had established contact with St. Benedict's Center and its director, Father Leonard Feeney, S.J. At the time the center was known for its large number of converts. Later Father Feeney and a number of his followers would adopt an extreme position on the salvation of non-Catholics, which would eventually lead to their ex-communication. Although there were as yet no overt signs of problems at St. Benedict's Center, Muzquiz was somewhat put off by the environment. He commented, "In time perhaps people can come from this center, and they certainly have affection for us, but we should begin with people who are less pious, if that's the right description for them."

FROM NEW YORK THEY TOOK A TRAIN to Chicago where they intended to open a center. Father Joseph said Mass for the first time in Chicago in the Church of St. Francis, at a side altar dedicated to Our Lady of Guadalupe. Muzquiz himself stayed in the rectory of St. Francis Church because priests at the time were expected to live in a rectory. Barredo was working in Enrico Fermi's laboratory at the University of Chicago, which was the most prestigious university in Chicago and one of the leading universities in the United States. He and the other three lay members of the Work rented four rooms near the university in the Harvard Hotel. "Despite its name," Muzquiz comments, "it was a modest place." The fact that they paid $1 a day for each room suggests that "modest" was a generous description.

Muzquiz met the others for dinner every evening. At first they went for dinner to a cafeteria or to one of the dining rooms at the University of Chicago. Although they ate together, they missed the warmth of eating at home so they decided to fix their own meals in their room. At first they bought cold cuts, but one day Sal bought raw tongue, thinking it was cooked. Rather than throw it out, they bought a hot plate and frying pan and began to cook, though none of them had any cooking experience. One day they forgot to turn off the hot plate, which was sitting on a suitcase when they left the room. The resulting small fire did little damage but almost got them thrown out of the hotel and put an end to their cooking in their rooms.

Whether they ate out or fixed something at home, after dinner they sat down for an informal family conversation they called a "get-together."[9] They talked about the events of the day, news

---

9. In Spain in the 1930s it was common for groups of friends to meet on a regular basis after dinner either in a bar or in one of their homes in what they called a *tertulia*. Building on this social custom, from the beginning of Opus Dei members of the Work have had *tertulias* in the living room of the center, usually after dinner. These informal conversations are an opportunity to relax, to get to know each other better, to enjoy each other's company and to exchange news about apostolic activities and other events. Muzquiz and the others who came to start Opus Dei in the United States adopted the term "get-together" to describe these family gatherings.

they had received in letters from members of the Work in Spain or Rome, people they had met, and plans for the future. Not long after they arrived, they received a postcard from Escrivá saying that he assumed they were settling into their new country and were speaking English among themselves. From that moment on, Ferigle recalled, "Father Joseph never spoke to me again in Spanish except in groups where there were people who knew no English."

During their early months in Chicago, Muzquiz and the others faced a formidable set of challenges. They had no money, knew hardly anyone, spoke little English, and were unfamiliar with the way of doing things in the United States. Faced with these challenges, Muzquiz had recourse first of all to prayer. He wrote to Escrivá at the end of March: "Every day I see more clearly what you have told us so often about the need for personal sanctity. I feel small and unworthy, but I see that our Lord loves me a great deal, and I want to love him a great deal." This is a recurring theme in Muzquiz's correspondence. Several weeks later he wrote: "When you asked me to go to the United States, one of the things that gave me most joy was the fact that I would necessarily have to live an intense life of faith and that there would be no danger of falling into lukewarmness. I don't correspond to all the graces I receive, but our Lord helps me a lot. I think it is good for me to have to ask for everything. When there is an organized apostolate, I run the danger of routine or of being absorbed by work. Here we have to expect everything from our Lord. I think that he and he alone has to move hearts to give themselves to him. He can move them whenever he wants. He makes us wait to test our confidence, for however long he wants. I tell our Lord that we need instruments for the apostolate, but that he knows better than we when they are needed."

During the month of May, as is the custom in Opus Dei, Father Joseph and the others intensified their prayer to Our Lady. He would have liked to make a simple pilgrimage to a shrine of Our Lady to honor her during May, but since he did not know of any shrines near Chicago, he settled for going with Barredo one Sunday to an Eastern Rite Catholic church to pray the Rosary in front of one of the icons of the Mother of God.

For Opus Dei to carry out its mission of serving the Church in the United States, it was essential to find young men and women who would dedicate their lives to God in Opus Dei and would try to put its spirit into practice and spread it to others. For that, a vital first step was to get to know young people whom God might be calling to this path of service to the Church. One place to do that was Calvert House, the Catholic Club at the University of Chicago. Muzquiz also contacted a number of Catholic high schools and in many cases found the priests and brothers anxious to help him meet students who might be interested in Opus Dei's message. At Marmion Academy, a military boarding high school run by the Benedictines, he gave talks to the Latin-American students as well as to the students studying Spanish. At Barredo's suggestion, he called unannounced the Dean of Mundelein College, Sister Mary Bernarda, who had translated a book from Spanish, and asked her to translate the bulletin about Zorzano's cause for canonization. This gave him an opportunity to explain Opus Dei and to ask her to talk about it with students who might be interested. A number of Dominicans, Franciscans, and Passionists, many of whom Barredo had met earlier and to whom he had talked about Opus Dei, also introduced people to Muzquiz.

Meeting people was only a first step. It was necessary to communicate to those they met that Opus Dei's spirit was not just an interesting theory but something to live in daily life. That was not easy. In the first place, Opus Dei's message of sanctity for lay people in the midst of the world was shockingly novel to American Catholics. Many of them went to Mass regularly but had little idea of what an interior life of prayer and sacrifice consists in, and even less idea that God might be asking them to lead such a life without becoming priests or nuns. Muzquiz told Escrivá: "We have to struggle against a terrible lack of formation. My fellow priests propose as the maximum goal in life for a young man to marry a Catholic girl."

The novelty of the message was compounded by difficulty in communicating in English. On Holy Thursday Ferigle accompanied a young man who had served in the Pacific at the end of World War II on visits to the Blessed Sacrament in a number of churches. He had to prolong each visit to give himself time to rehearse in English the things he wanted to tell his companion about Opus Dei as they walked to the next church.

The size of the city presented another obstacle. One of the students they met was studying journalism at Northwestern University in Evanston, just north of Chicago. That put him at more than an hour's distance by subway from the University of Chicago. Although this was an extreme case, many people they met lived far enough away that it was difficult to maintain regular contact with them. On the positive side, Muzquiz found that people were good about keeping appointments and had quite a bit of time free on Saturdays and Sundays.

At the end of May it seemed that Mary might have answered Father Joseph's fervent prayers for American members. A freshman at the University of Illinois in Champaign-Urbana who had met Barredo at Marmion Academy came to Chicago to ask him about Spanish universities. When Barredo told him about Opus Dei he became enthused and immediately decided that God was calling him to the Work. A week later, he returned to Chicago and asked to be admitted as a member of the Work. "We don't want to get our hopes too high," Muzquiz wrote to Escrivá, "but it seems like he could be the first stone." For a while he came to Chicago every weekend to be with the members of the Work and to receive formation, but by the end of July Muzquiz concluded they had been overly optimistic. It would be difficult for him to persevere unless he moved to Chicago where he could be in close contact with members of the Work and learn to live its spirit. When that did not happen, he gradually dropped out of sight; years later he renewed his contact with Opus Dei and became a cooperator.

AT THE SAME TIME THAT HE WORKED to meet people and explain Opus Dei to them, Father Joseph needed to obtain official Church approval for Opus Dei to carry out its apostolic activities in Chicago. He assumed that this would be no problem. During their visit to Cardinal Stritch in 1948, Casciaro and Barredo had gotten the impression that the Cardinal was anxious to have Opus Dei begin working in the diocese. The decision to begin in Chicago rather than somewhere else in the United States was inspired in part by that belief.

As soon as he arrived in Chicago, Muzquiz requested an appointment with Cardinal Strich, but the Cardinal was in Florida and even once he returned it was not easy to see him. When Father Joseph finally met him for the first time in mid-March, he discovered that Barredo's and Casciaro's limited command of English and of American customs had led them to misinterpret courteous pleasantries as an invitation to begin working in the diocese. The Cardinal asked for a written report, and refused to be drawn into further conversation.

Father Joseph was disconcerted by the cold reception he received and by the Cardinal's apparent lack of interest in hearing about the spirit and the apostolates of Opus Dei, but working with the other members of the Work, he prepared the report. He expected a speedy response, but weeks went by and none arrived. Eventually Muzquiz came to the conclusion that the Cardinal's reticence was due to fear that they were going to ask him for money. Although financial help was certainly needed, Muzquiz made it clear to the chancellor of the diocese that they were not asking for help and would raise on their own the money they needed to acquire a house. That seemed to clear the air considerably. Nonetheless numerous phone calls and another visit to the Cardinal were required before he finally gave his blessing in writing in mid-July.

ROOMS IN THE HARVARD HOTEL WERE NOT an adequate base for Opus Dei's apostolic activities. In Spain and other countries where universities had few or no dormitories and students often had difficulty finding suitable housing, Opus Dei had opened a number of student residences near major universities. They offered a homelike environment, an atmosphere of serious study, and an opportunity for those who wished to receive the sacraments and Christian formation. The residences had greatly facilitated Opus Dei's apostolate with students. From the beginning, Muzquiz and the others planned to open a similar student residence in Chicago.

At first they were unsure of where to locate it. The University of Chicago Catholic had few Catholic students and a high proportion of foreign students, while Opus Dei's priority for the moment was to work with American Catholics. On the other hand, Chicago was the most prestigious university in the city, and Barredo already knew a number of people there. The warm reception Father Joseph received at the University of Chicago Catholic Club helped dispel his doubts about the best place to begin.

Although they had no money to buy even the smallest of houses, Muzquiz and the others began to look for a house near the University of Chicago large enough to permit them to open a residence that would be not merely a dormitory but a home and a center of cultural and spiritual activities. Father Joseph was convinced that they could cover operating expenses with six to eight residents and confident they could find them, but he had no idea how they could put together enough money for the purchase. Nonetheless, he contacted a real estate agent named Tom Cremin for help in locating a house. When Cremin asked how they planned to pay for it, Muzquiz and Ferigle merely said they would work out something. Cremin was astonished, but sufficiently impressed by their confidence in divine providence that he took them to see a number of houses.

The only suitable building for sale near the university was a fifteen-room brick house at 5544 S. Woodlawn Avenue, just a few blocks from the campus. When Cremin asked Father Joseph if he could make a down payment of $25,000, Muzquiz thought he was asking if they could pay a total price of $25,000. Although they only had $2,000 at the time, he said yes. Later he clarified that the most they could put down would be $10,000. Sometime later he dropped that to $7,000, and eventually he confessed that they could only come up with $5,000 as a down payment. Cremin was so impressed with Father Joseph's sincerity, innocence, and acceptance of God's will that he offered to donate his entire commission to help them put together the down payment. The seller's agent, convinced that the credit of a Catholic priest was good, offered to give them a first mortgage for two-thirds of the value of the house, but that left the other third to be paid.

Muzquiz disliked fund raising and did not consider himself good at it, but this did not prevent him from throwing himself into the task. Having just arrived in the country, they didn't know anyone who could make donations. Muzquiz spent many days in downtown Chicago, looking for potential donors. He began to say Mass at a downtown church where he could meet business people after Mass. One gave him $100 of his own and $100 from a friend. He also referred him to a third person who gave him another $50. Father Joseph was grateful for these contributions, but it was going to take more than $100 donations to pay for the house.

A Cuban student at the University of Chicago introduced Muzquiz to a lawyer friend who he thought could help. The lawyer said he couldn't help, but he in turn introduced Muzquiz to his cousin, John O'Shaughnessy, who liked things Spanish and was taken with the idea of a student residence. O'Shaughnessy gave them a second mortgage on extremely favorable terms. With O'Shaughnessy's help and small contributions from various sources, little by little Muzquiz assembled much of what he needed, but the work was slow and difficult. He wrote to Escrivá: "Either I'm not much good at this, or people here are hard to convince. In either case, things go slowly." At the end of June a Spanish friend of Casciaro's donated enough money to enable them to sign the purchase contract and do a few of the most essential things to make the house habitable. By early July the last major obstacles had been overcome and the details of the deal set.

In addition to purchasing the house, they needed to furnish it and build an oratory. Muzquiz appears not to have worried much about furniture, but he was concerned about the oratory, which is the heart of every Opus Dei center. Building and equipping a suitable oratory would be expensive. The problem was partially solved by two elderly sisters, Clara and Sophie Daleiden, whose names Muzquiz had gotten from a priest friend of Del Portillo. He had imagined that they were wealthy women, but when he went to visit them for the first time, he was surprised to find himself in a very modest neighborhood:

I looked at the paper with the address several times to make sure I was not mistaken. When I made my way up to the top floor — the third — I realized I was in the right place. They received me cordially and told me that the church goods store on the ground floor was run by a nephew of theirs. I went to see them several times and occasionally I said Mass in a small oratory they had. . . .

When the contract for the acquisition of the house which would become the residence was being drawn up, I prepared with Sal a little speech to explain to them that we were going to start a student residence at the University of Chicago and that we wanted to have an oratory with the Blessed Sacrament where we could say Mass, have days of recollection etc. In the second part of the speech, I planned to say that since we came from Spain, which is a poor country, we had no money and would appreciate anything they could give us, even if only a stole. But the second part proved unnecessary. As soon as I mentioned the oratory, they said, "We will take care of the altar and the tabernacle."

FATHER JOSEPH TOOK ADVANTAGE of the period of calm between working out the final details and closing on the house to travel to Mexico to change his tourist visa for a resident visa. The trip also gave him an opportunity to talk at length with Father Pedro Casciaro. The chance to talk with another experienced member of the Work must have been especially welcome. Collegial government is a fundamental principle in Opus Dei. Muzquiz had learned from Escrivá that no one should make important decisions about the activities of Opus Dei alone. As head of Opus Dei in the United States, Muzquiz followed this principle diligently, consulting the other members of the Work about the decisions he had to make. As someone who worked with him in Opus Dei's governing body in the United States, the Regional Commission, notes, "he always took the opinions of the other directors into account before making decisions even if, at times, his own convictions were quite strong as a result of his long years of experience and having worked closely with St. Josemaría. He had clear ideas as to what was in accordance with the spirit of Opus Dei and what was not; but never failed to let the others express their opinions."

Nonetheless, especially in the early days in Chicago, he must have felt keenly the need to talk with another older member of the Work. The only other experienced person in Chicago, Barredo, was an intelligent scientist and a faithful and dedicated member of the Work, but not particularly gifted for practical affairs. The others were all quite young and still relatively new in Opus Dei. Ferigle, whom Muzquiz seems to have identified early on as the person on whom he could most rely, was still only twenty-six-years old and had belonged to Opus Dei for less than five years.

Opus Dei had only recently been approved by the Holy See. Practical questions about its status in the Church, which had not yet been fully answered, came up with some frequency in dealing with Cardinal Stritch and other ecclesiastical authorities. In addition, many decisions had to be made about how to begin developing Opus Dei in a country very different from Spain: In what terms should they cast Opus Dei's message to make it more comprehensible to Americans? Which of the things that struck them as odd in the life of their new country were simply different from what they were accustomed to and which were defects of the American character, which they should try to help people overcome? What age group should they concentrate their apostolic efforts on?

Muzquiz would have liked to be able to consult the General Council, Opus Dei's international governing body, and especially Escrivá, about these and other questions, but often that was impossible. Escrivá had established his residence in Rome in 1946, but still spent long periods of time in Spain. The General Council was still located in Madrid. Many questions had to be answered immediately. For issues that were less pressing, airmail service was quick and inexpensive, but apart from the intrinsic limitations of writing as opposed to face-to-face communication, the mail censorship exercised by the Franco government made Muzquiz reluctant to use mail for some questions. Transatlantic telephone was quick, but it was still expensive and also subject to censorship.

Muzquiz's correspondence reflects his concern over having to make important decisions without an opportunity for consultation. He must have been relieved to receive a letter in which Escrivá said: "You have done very well, Jose Luis, in all the things you have done. You have interpreted my wishes perfectly making decisions as you have made them. . . . Act, Jose Luis, with complete freedom after hearing your brothers." Nonetheless, it must have been a great relief to be able to talk at length with Casciaro and to compare notes with him.

∼ 6.

FIRST CENTERS AND MEMBERS

ON SUNDAY, AUGUST 21, 1949, THEY RECEIVED the keys and took possession of the house. They could count on Barredo's fellowship, the scholarship that Ferigle had received from the Illinois Institute of Technology where he was pursuing a doctorate in physics, and small amounts that the others were able to bring in through scholarships or work, but that was barely sufficient to make payments on the mortgage and on the loan from O'Shaughnessey. As Muzquiz wrote, they were essentially "broke," and there was no money to buy furniture. Nonetheless they moved in immediately.

They were pleased to find around the house a few old beds, a large dining room table, a smaller table that Father Joseph used as a portable altar to celebrate Mass, and a few wooden boxes they used to supplement the one chair they found in the house, which was immediately dubbed "The Chair." Little by little, various people they had met gave them used furniture, but the process was slow and they were nowhere near having enough to furnish a large house and turn it into a student residence.

Several people mentioned a Mrs. Bramsfield, an active and generous person whose many contacts they thought could help them in locating furniture. One day someone introduced Muzquiz to her outside church after Mass: "This is Father Muzquiz who comes from Spain. He is starting a student residence at the University of Chicago and needs furniture." Mrs. Bramsfield asked him what he needed, probably thinking it would be a question of a couple of chairs or a table or two. She was somewhat taken aback, when he responded "everything," but she soon visited Woodlawn and quickly organized a committee of women who tackled the task of furnishing the future residence, largely with items donated by older couples who were moving from large houses to apartments or smaller houses.

Muzquiz joked in a letter to Escrivá: "You would think that to furnish a house you would need to buy furniture. Well here it's just the opposite: if things continue going as they have, we will have to begin selling. We already have four radios and three dining room tables . . . . We still need some things, but they will arrive. I don't think there has been a single day this month in which we didn't receive something. One day it is a package of sheets or blankets or some curtains or a rug. Another day a furniture truck stops and unloads an armoire or a table. Yet another day someone fills the pantry with canned goods or a lady comes to tell us she has sent the table she had in her living room. It is all very amusing and very American."

In a more serious tone, he added: "We are glad to begin this way and to have the furniture, linens, etc. come bit by bit from people who take an interest in helping us. It is wonderful that in this country, which we hope will eventually support activities elsewhere, our Lord has arranged things so that from the beginning we live real poverty and are in no danger of 'Americanizing' ourselves as has happened to so many people."

One of the features of American life that Muzquiz found most puzzling and hard to adjust to was the lack of domestic help. After spending the night with the family of a law professor, he told Escrivá in amazement that "I almost helped them prepare the meals and wash the dishes." Shortly after moving in to Woodlawn he commented on the fact that their neighbor, a professor of medicine at the University of Chicago, had a nice house, but that he and his family not only did their own cooking, but took out the garbage.

MORE URGENT THAN FURNISHING THE HOUSE was converting a second floor room into a fitting oratory where the Blessed Sacrament could be reserved. Muzquiz vividly recalled the joy with which Escrivá left the Blessed Sacrament for the first time in the tabernacle of a new Opus Dei center in Madrid. That oratory had a painting of the disciples of Emmaus with Christ. Inscribed on the altar were their words, "Stay with us, for it is toward evening and the day is now far spent" (Lk 24:29). Commenting on that phrase, Escrivá had said: "Without you, Lord, everything is darkness. With you, on the other hand, all is light." The conviction that Christ's presence in the tabernacle would fill the house with light and joy moved Muzquiz to finish a provisional oratory as quickly as possible.

They were shocked at the cost of hiring painters, electricians, and other workers. Coming from a country where skilled labor was cheap and doing it yourself was virtually unknown, they had no skill or experience in remodeling, but they made up for their lack of knowledge with enthusiasm and good will. They recruited a number of boys they had met to help with painting, and a little more than three weeks after moving in, a temporary oratory was finished. On September 15, 1949, the feast of Our Lady of Sorrows, Father Joseph celebrated Mass in the oratory and for the first time left the Blessed Sacrament reserved in the tabernacle of a center of Opus Dei in the United States.

Muzquiz was delighted to have Christ present in the tabernacle of the center. "We are very happy to have our Lord at home with us. We don't know how to thank Him for having wanted to stay among us. Here far away one notices even more the need to unburden oneself with Him and to thank him for everything he has given us and is going to give us." The first oratory was merely provisional and they immediately turned to preparing a permanent one to replace it. They found someone to donate candlesticks. Another person sent painters and a third had the floor carpeted. During December they worked feverishly on the project and were able to have Midnight Mass in the new oratory on Christmas.

When Father Joseph celebrated Mass or Benediction, his love of God was evident in the devotion and care with which he treated Our Lord in the Blessed Sacrament. People noticed the piety, recollection, and fervor with which he held the monstrance to his breast. A woman who normally used a missal at Mass but forgot to bring it one day, was so moved by Father Joseph's celebration of Mass that she concluded God had permitted her to forget her missal so that she might come to love the Mass more by observing how he celebrated.

Similarly, the love of God and conviction with which he preached moved people. He was not a talented orator, but people had the impression of being in the presence of a holy person whose only goals were to do the will of God and to live the spirit of Opus Dei. He brought people to God through his piety, the warmth of his recollections of St. Josemaría, and his affection for him. Even someone who found some of his mannerisms irritating was won over by his evident love of God. His direct simplicity helped people, perhaps particularly young people, to grasp the importance of personal struggle to work on a particular virtue or point.

Father Joseph and the others worked steadily at putting together a group of young men whom they could help to develop a solid interior life of prayer and sacrifice, some of whom might receive from God a call to Opus Dei. By the end of October, they had a large enough group to be able to have a meditation and benediction of the Blessed Sacrament on Saturday evenings, and they were busy organizing classes of spiritual formation patterned on the circles Muzquiz had attended himself in the 1930s. Father Joseph commented: "The spiritual life is something new for them. It is a joy, however, to sow the seed, and when it begins to develop the harvest will be enormous. We are happy and we are beginning to see palpable fruits in some of the boys." At the end of their first year in the United States, Muzquiz reflected on the experience gained thus far. He and the other members of the Work had explained the vocation to Opus Dei in some depth to more than forty young men who they thought might be called to the Work. Writing to Escrivá, Muzquiz commented: "The young men continue not to respond. I don't know if it is because they have a different mentality, that they have received poor formation, or if we still don't know how to deal with them. We are filled with peace by your saying that our work is very pleasing to our Lord and that the fruits will come soon. I think at times that perhaps things don't work out because our Lord is not pleased with us, but I try to reject that thought as a temptation. When I see the enthusiasm and the effort of some of my brothers I feel sure that our Lord will soon do great things in Chicago." He concluded that although many young American Catholics were good and had faith and piety, their piety was often superficial and without sacrifice. In most cases he thought it would be necessary to look for future members among quite young people who had not yet been deformed by the environment.

CONTRARY TO MUZQUIZ'S EXPECTATIONS, THE FIRST American vocation would be a mature man who had served in the Navy at the end of World War II. Richard Rieman learned about Opus Dei from Father Mann, a Redemptorist, whom Father Joseph met during a meeting of priests at the University of Notre Dame. In June 1950 Rieman, a twenty-four-year-old former Navy aviator, was grappling with a vocational question and wanted to make a retreat. He called Father Joseph and made an appointment to talk with him.

At the time, Rieman was working from 10 a.m. to 10 p.m. seven days a week as the technical director of the mounted units of "Frontiers of Freedom," a summer show with a cast of 150 presented on the lake front at the Chicago Fair.[10] Muzquiz was not about to let Rieman's schedule be an obstacle. He suggested a "modified retreat." Instead of going home in the evening after work, Rieman would sleep at Woodlawn. In the morning, during a half-hour before Mass, Father Joseph would give a meditation or someone would read points for meditation from Escrivá's book *The Way*. After Mass and breakfast, Rieman would have a get-together with Muzquiz and other members of the Work and then go off to work.

When he first arrived at Woodlawn, Rieman made an excellent impression on Muzquiz who described him as "one-hundred-percent American: a Navy pilot during the War, athletic and cheerful." Rieman's character, apostolic drive, and spirit of service soon led Muzquiz and Ferigle to think that God might be calling him to Opus Dei. Rieman himself started asking Father Joseph to allow him to join. Muzquiz was aware, however, that on previous occasions he might have been overly enthusiastic and acted too quickly. He wrote to Escrivá asking whether they should allow Rieman to join immediately. In the note he "tried to be as objective as possible . . . " but added, "really he seems marvelous to us in every way. . . . I don't want my heart to run away with me, but the truth is I'd be very sad if it weren't possible for him to fit in." Several days later, returning to the same subject, he added, "It seems clear to us [that he should be allowed to join the Work], but we will be happy to do whatever you tell us. If this one fails and doesn't work out, God will send others."

One day while they were waiting for a reply from Rome, Ferigle mentioned to Rieman that they needed some bricks to square off the opening they had made in an outside wall for a new door. They had located the necessary bricks not far away

---

10. The hour-long show traced American history, stressing the role of freedom in the nation's development. It had over $2 million of equipment ranging from the first McCormick reaper to a jet plane, as well as the stagecoaches, cowboys, and fifty longhorn steers that were Rieman's responsibility.

but didn't have a car to pick them up. Rieman's stock dropped sharply in Ferigle's and Muzquiz's eyes when he didn't offer to pick up the bricks or to lend them his car. It dropped even further when next day he did not show up for the meditation or for Mass. Shortly after breakfast, however, he arrived with a trunk full of bricks, and his stock shot back up.

Having received Escrivá's approval, on July 14 Ferigle explained to Rieman in greater depth what it meant to serve God and the Church as a member of Opus Dei. Rieman immediately said yes, but Ferigle told him that he should think about it more before deciding. On July 15, the anniversary of Isidoro's Zorzano's death, Rieman wrote a letter officially asking to be admitted as a member of Opus Dei.

From Ferigle's comments about Muzquiz's trips to New York, Washington, and Boston and about the many people he was in contact with, Rieman had concluded that there were many American members of Opus Dei. He was surprised when the first letter he received from Escrivá spoke about his "blessed responsibility" as the first. He took that responsibility seriously. Soon he began bringing young men who worked at the show to Woodlawn for Mass and confession, days of recollection, or to help fix up and paint the house. Some of them he invited to join him in saying the Rosary on the shore of Lake Michigan between one performance and the next. At first there were only three or four people, but by the end of the summer the number saying the Rosary grew to twenty. Several regulars were not Catholic and one was studying to be a Lutheran minister. By the beginning of the 1950–51 school year, when Rieman was a student at De Paul University, enough people were attending activities at Woodlawn to organize three circles, one for high school students, one for college students, and a third for recent graduates.

Muzquiz's zeal and his love of travel led him to follow up on possible leads even in out-of-the-way places. Occasionally Rieman accompanied him. In early fall 1950 they went by car with

Ferigle to Minneapolis/St. Paul, along the way visiting people in a number of small towns and cities and on the way back stopping in Dubuque, Iowa and Madison, Wisconsin. In November, Father Joseph received a visit from a young woman living in Manitowoc, Wisconsin, a small town on the shores of Lake Michigan about 180 miles north of Chicago. At her request, he traveled to Manitowoc to give a talk about Opus Dei to a group of women. On the same trip, he gave talks or visited priests in Fond du Lac, Green Bay, Appleton, and Milwaukee.

The increase in the numbers of people attending means of formation and receiving spiritual direction from Father Joseph soon seemed to pay off in a flurry of new members. Muzquiz observed: "What moves them to make up their mind is the love of God and generosity. The environment in which they live here is in some ways very different, but deep down souls are the same, or at least there are many with desires to really give themselves to God."

Between Christmas 1950 and early January 1951 five young men asked to be admitted to Opus Dei. The oldest was a Woodlawn resident pursuing a Ph.D. in music, another was a freshman at the University of Chicago, and the other three were high school students who had worked with Rieman during the summer. Early in February another University of Chicago student joined Opus Dei. During March three more asked to be admitted.

By summer 1951, however, three of them had turned back, and eventually only Rieman persevered. Looking back on the events, Muzquiz saw a parallel with what had happened to Escrivá in the early days of Opus Dei: "It seems that our Lord wanted us to tread the same path. Those first members, some of which came on feast days, were like 'a thimbleful of honey,' even though later on 'they escaped like eels.'"

Father Joseph's ardent desire to spread Opus Dei in the service of the Church and his warm affection for the people who joined the Work gave him great determination in trying to help them go forward. He was prepared to go to great lengths to help anyone who found himself facing special difficulties in responding to God's call. On one occasion, at Escrivá's suggestion, he traveled urgently to Venezuela to talk with a member of the Work who was vacillating. Muzquiz's warm interest helped him overcome his doubts. Similarly, on another occasion, he interrupted a trip to New York and Washington to return to Chicago to try to help a young man who was going through an especially difficult period.

THE FIRST THREE WOMEN OF OPUS DEI arrived in Chicago from Spain in May 1950 led by Nisa Gónzalez Guzmán, an accomplished tennis player and down-hilll skier who had joined Opus Dei in 1941. Later that year they were joined by Blanca Dorda and Margarita Barturen. Initially they did not have a corporate apostolic activity of their own. While perfecting their English, getting their bearings in the country, meeting people, and laying the foundations of their future apostolic activities, they lived in an independent apartment at the rear of the building on Woodlawn Avenue and did the cooking and housekeeping for the newly established student residence.[11]

Rieman introduced his cousin, Pat Lind, to the new arrivals in October 1950. Although the young women who had come from Spain still had some difficulty communicating in English, they hit it off well with her. Pat began to visit them regularly, and celebrated New Year's Eve 1951 with them. On June 19, 1951, she wrote a letter to Escrivá asking to be admitted as a member of Opus Dei, thereby becoming the first North American woman member.

Muzquiz and Escrivá were anxious for the women of Opus Dei to have a building of their own where they could carry out a

---

11. So important did Escrivá consider the contribution that some women of Opus Dei make to its apostolate creating a family environment in both women and men's centers, taking care of cooking and cleaning that he often called it "the apostolate of apostolates." Nonetheless, after the experience in Chicago he decided that the women of Opus Dei should not work in a new country or a new city without having from the beginning a corporate apostolic activity of their own.

corporate apostolic activity with women, but another year went by before Muzquiz was able to acquire for the women's branch a large house a few blocks from Woodlawn. Nisa Guzmán, one of the first women members of Opus Dei, said she liked it better than any other house she had ever seen.

Amazingly, Muzquiz pulled off the purchase with no money, not even for the down payment. He convinced the owners—a Catholic couple named Cavanaugh whose children had grown up and left home—to sell the house along with many furnishings for $47,000 but to contribute $17,000 of the purchase price back to the buyers so they could use it as the down payment. Muzquiz found it "amusing" to buy a house "without a single dollar of our own; two mortgages and a loan from the seller's bank backed by the seller's guarantee. As soon as the paper work is done, the seller will give us a check for $17,000 with which to pay off the loan" whose proceeds were used as the down payment.

BY THE END OF 1951, ONLY TWO YEARS AFTER the first members of Opus Dei arrived in the United States with no money and a rudimentary command of English, both the men's and the women's branches were installed in substantial centers and in touch with growing numbers of people. Opus Dei was still a tiny presence in the United States, but thanks to Father Joseph's prayer, sacrifice, and effort, it had begun to put down roots and to reach out to all types of people, men and women, single and married, laymen and priests.

~ 7.

RETREATS

ONCE THE REMODELING OF WOODLAWN had progressed far enough, Muzquiz organized a retreat for a group of high school boys from St. Mel's, a school run by the Christian Brothers. It began on January 30, 1952, and was soon followed by many other retreats for boys of this age.

For a number of years, three-day retreats for groups of ten to twelve students were the principal focus of Father Joseph's apostolic activity in Chicago. The retreats were a way of getting to know more students and teaching them the rudiments of the spirit of Opus Dei, especially the sanctification of studies and the rest of daily life.

At times, especially during Lent, Father Joseph would preach several retreats a week. His schedule was grueling. Often he finished one retreat in the morning and began another the same afternoon. In each retreat, in addition to saying Mass, preaching five or six half-hour meditations a day, and hearing confessions, he tried to have at least one personal conversation with each participant.

Those conversations were the heart of the retreat for many of the boys. They were effective because Father Joseph was so thoroughly a man of God and a priest. One person observed, "He had not the slightest hint of pretension about him, and neither did he show any particular interest in talking as an 'educated man' or as one able to discuss current issues and cultural topics. . . . He didn't talk about himself at all." Indeed, it was hard to see that he had any interests except those associated with his dedication and zeal. Yet this zeal was gentle and somehow so blended with his personality and the immediate situation that it didn't show as zeal.

Another person completes the picture: "His cheerfulness, his smile, his words, everything about him, inspired confidence. He was the sort of person whom you would tell, with great naturalness, the most intimate aspects of your life." Because of his accepting smile, a professional violinist found that "it was easy for me to tell him what was on my mind, what was in my soul. He remembered details of our family life and specific members of the family. He was a true father. . . . He made me welcome, never creating the impression that he had other, pressing duties."

Muzquiz was so pleasant to be with and so authentic that he put people at ease and made them feel comfortable opening their hearts to him. He was a great listener and also had great understanding. A friend describes his attitude as "*expectant* as if he was always ready to help you in whatever way you needed." He was so simple and direct that he had, as it were, perfected the art of easily and naturally speaking of spiritual things and touching souls without any great ado. Talking with him moved people to greater generosity and a desire to know God and serve him better. Many found that his mere presence was a strong invitation to pray, to communicate with God.

Many of the students who attended the retreats were enthusiastic about the experience and spread the word to their classmates. Soon boys were coming from eight or ten high schools. Many lived far from Woodlawn, but Muzquiz and the other members of the Work who helped with the retreats, especially Rieman and Ferigle, tried to stay in contact with those who showed more interest by organizing circles near their schools. In March twenty boys came to Woodlawn for an all-night vigil of the Blessed Sacrament. Later they invited some of the boys to teach catechism in poor neighborhoods. Helping the boys prepare the catechism classes provided an opportunity to see them on a regular basis, thereby helping them deepen their own faith while gauging their generosity of spirit.

The principal of Alvernia High School, a member of the School Sisters of St. Francis, learned from the principal of St. Mel's about the retreats being offered for boys at Woodlawn, she immediately expressed interest in organizing similar retreats for girls from her school. She also invited Father Joseph to address an association of principals of girls' Catholic high schools to tell them about the retreats. No sooner had the women of Opus Dei occupied their house (Kenwood Residence) than they began offering retreats both for married women and for girls from fifteen different schools.

Muzquiz found himself giving several retreats a week for high school girls in addition to his other duties. One week in March 1953 there was a retreat for girls that ran from Sunday to Wednesday morning, a day of recollection for ladies on Wednesday afternoon, a retreat for girls from Wednesday evening to Saturday morning, another retreat that started Saturday and finished Sunday, and a day of recollection Sunday morning for girls. At times he would preach concurrent retreats, one for boys at Woodlawn and another for girls at Kenwood, giving twelve half-hour meditations each day and traveling back and forth between the two centers six times a day.

Father Joseph saw the retreats as a service to the participants and rejoiced at their resolutions to live a more intense Christian life and to try to bring their friends and classmates closer to Christ. He was anxious, however, for some of them to hear God's call to Opus Dei and disappointed when it did not happen. In May 1952 he wrote to Escrivá, "Father, I am concerned about the lack of vocations. Everything else, thanks be to God, is going well." He attributed the difficulty in finding new members "in part to lack of formation, in part to the distances in Chicago [which made it difficult to maintain regular contact with young people] and in part to the fact that all or almost all of them—even those from families with money—work after school as messengers, clerks, or what have you, which leaves them little free time." But, he added, "We continue sowing, and it is a joy to sow, even if the fruits take time in coming."

~8.

SUPPORTING ESCRIVÁ'S
EFFORTS IN ROME

IN 1947 OPUS DEI ACQUIRED A PIECE of property in a residential area of Rome on which to build its international headquarters. The construction of Villa Tevere, as the complex would be called, began in 1949 but would take more than a decade to complete. Despite his dislike of fund raising, his lack of contacts, and the pressing need for money to remodel and furnish Woodlawn and Kenwood residences, Muzquiz worked diligently to raise money for the project.

In January 1950, responding to a request for help from Don Alvaro Del Portillo,[12] Muzquiz wrote to Escrivá: "I was glad to receive Alvaro's note, and I would be even happier to be able to help seriously. As you know, Father, you have here a quite useless son, but for fund raising I am a disaster. We are making progress on furniture and decorations, but I've had little success in raising cash. I have a few leads. I've been following a

_____

12. It is common in Spain to refer to priests by their first name preceded by the respectful title "don." I observe that custom in some quotations and occasionally in referring to Alvaro Del Portillo, Escrivá's close collaborator and first successor, who was generally called in Opus Dei "Don Alvaro."

number of them for several months without much result, but *in verbo autem tuo laxabo rete* [at your word I will lower the net. Lk 5:5]. Father, you'll see how everything will work out and how your American children will be able to really help what has to be the heart and head of the Work in the whole world."

A few days later, Escrivá insisted again on the need for help with the construction of Villa Tevere:

> Just a few words to ask you to pray insistently for our work here. We are writing to you again to see if you can find someone who will help economically with these buildings which are an indispensable instrument for the whole Work. I insist. We are really in a jam. So far we have resolved the problems with human means of credits and mortgages—on which we are reaching the end of the line—and with true miracles which our Lord works when he wants to.
>
> I am aware of your efforts to go forward with everything you are doing there, but I wouldn't feel right if I didn't tell you all about the enormous financial concerns we have here. Pray, and if you don't achieve anything "humanly" for these buildings in Rome, don't worry. In any case, nothing—none of your efforts—will be sterile.

Muzquiz traveled to Milwaukee to meet with the son of the owner of a large company. The young man, who was much interested in mysticism and contemplation, had given away much of his fortune to monasteries and convents of contemplative orders. He didn't give Father Joseph any money, but did give him a letter of introduction to a New York Catholic millionaire.

Although he had no appointment and no certainty of getting one, Muzquiz took the train to New York to see him. He was told that the man was out of the country, but was expected to return in a few days. While waiting for him to return to New York, Father Joseph made a brief trip to Washington where he visited the Apostolic Delegate and had dinner with the Spanish ambassador. He also gave a talk about Opus Dei to a small group of Georgetown University students, friends of a student whom Barredo had met several years earlier. When he finally saw the millionaire back in New York, he told him that he was committed to building several Trappist monasteries. He could only give him $1,000 but said he would send another $500 soon and held out the hope that in the future he might be able to help in a more substantial way.

In May 1950 Muzquiz returned to New York to try once again to get money. He stayed in the home of the person he had visited before, who turned out to be interested primarily in making films about Fatima and in distributing music. Through him Muzquiz met the chairman of the board of a large corporation, but nothing tangible came of that meeting either.

Father Joseph intensified his prayer, asking "our Lord to make us see how we can help more with the house in Rome. I don't know if I lack daring or what," he told Escrivá, "but things don't work out." No possibility was too remote for him to try. He traveled to New York again to see if he could interest a New York bank in guaranteeing a loan that the members of Opus Dei in Colombia hoped to obtain, only to be told that U.S. banks had no interest in the project. He also studied the way to approach a wealthy Spanish businessman who had been repeatedly divorced and drank heavily. He would have no sympathy with the religious aspects of the project in Rome, but Muzquiz hoped he might be interested in its educational and cultural ramifications. He told Del Portillo, "It's a question of really praying hard and of our Lord's working the miracle we are hoping for."

Although unsuccessful in finding people who would give large amounts of money, Muzquiz worked diligently to locate other ways of helping. He convinced the owners of a bakery to donate 100 pounds of flour a week and another person to pay for shipping it as far as New York. To get it from there to Rome, he turned to the National Catholic Welfare Conference, which was still sending large amounts of post-war relief aid to

Italy. When ladies who attended the first reception held at the women's center in Chicago contributed $500, Muzquiz decided to send it to Rome. "Although lately we have had a lot of problems and debts, we feel that the first collection taken up in the women's house should go to Rome," he said. Shortly thereafter he decided to increase the mortgage on Woodlawn and send the money to Rome. He passed on suggestions received from friends for raising money from large numbers of small donors by "selling bricks" for $5 each and other similar devices, although he said he personally found them "ridiculous." Escrivá was impressed by Muzquiz's efforts and generosity despite the meager results.

Even when Muzquiz's initial contact with someone was to ask for money, he tried not only to win financial support but to bring the person closer to God. One of the people he approached for money was a successful Spanish businessman established in the United States who had not practiced his faith for years. Thanks to his dealings with Father Joseph he not only returned to the sacraments but began to practice mental prayer and say the Rosary. When he was diagnosed with incurable cancer, he sent Muzquiz plane tickets so he could visit him in Florida. During Father Joseph's visit, he told him that he was happy and serene, thanks to the Work, and anxious for it to grow so many other people could find the peace and serenity he had found.

THE HOLY SEE HAD GIVEN ITS INITIAL approval to Opus Dei in 1947, but in 1950 Escrivá was anxious to obtain definitive approval. Part of the process would be to present letters of support from bishops in different countries. Muzquiz took to heart the task of obtaining the letters. He traveled to Dubuque, Iowa, Springfield, Illinois, and Toronto, Canada to see bishops whom he had not met before but who had been mentioned to him by friends. In Dubuque he found that the bishop was in Florida. In Springfield he had a long and cordial conversation, but the bishop, who knew hardly anything about Opus Dei prior to Muzquiz's visit, was unwilling to write a letter. Other efforts were more successful. Thanks to Father Joseph's visits, Cardinal Stritch of Chicago and one of his auxiliary bishops, as well as the bishops of Madison, Wisconsin, and Lafayette, Indiana wrote letters. Father Joseph also obtained letters from the archbishop of Toronto and the archbishop of Panama City, who happened to be visiting the United States at the time.

IN 1948 OPUS DEI HAD OPENED AN INTERNATIONAL center of formation called the Roman College of the Holy Cross. There members would study philosophy and theology and learn the spirit of Opus Dei directly from the founder. Some would be ordained priests of Opus Dei, and all of them would become much better equipped to live their own calling and to spread Opus Dei's spirit to others. In 1952 Escrivá suggested that Muzquiz think about Americans who could go to Rome. Father Joseph immediately began making plans. Escrivá was pleased at Muzquiz's prompt response but warned against moving too quickly before the people had demonstrated that they had "firm, proven vocations."

In fall 1954 Muzquiz sent Dick Rieman and one other American to Rome. The following year he was able to send a larger group including Jim Albrecht, Edmund Hernandez, and René Schatteman. By Christmas 1955, a total of seven male members from the United States were there. That same year Patricia Lind and Theresa Wilson became the first women from the United States to go to Opus Dei's international center of formation for women, the Roman College of Holy Mary. The pace continued and even quickened in the following years. For the 1956 school year, nine Americans arrived in the Roman College of the Holy Cross, including Robert Buccciarrelli, Chris Schmitt, Malcolm Kennedy, and George Rossman. They were followed in 1957 by another six, including Bradley Arturi and Mike Curtin. Heading to Rome for a number of years when they were just beginning their professional careers or still studying at the university might have seemed imprudent or even crazy, but Father Joseph was confident of God's providence.

Sending a high proportion of the American members of the Work to Rome for formation involved serious sacrifices for Muzquiz as well as for the young men who pulled up stakes to go. It deprived him of people who could help Opus Dei spread in the United States. He said in a 1956 letter: "We would like to send many more, but we have to hold back a minimum who can act as directors and who can reinforce the Regional Commission. The majority of those we have left joined the Work only recently." With few exceptions, the centers were staffed almost exclusively by people who had joined Opus Dei only a short while before.

In addition to the absence of badly needed personnel, sending people to Rome involved financial hardship. Money was needed for travel to Rome and for scholarships to support the students while they were there. Moreover, in the case of people who were already working professionally, Opus Dei's centers were now deprived of an important source of economic support.

Despite the obvious drawbacks, Muzquiz was convinced of the value of sending people to Rome. There they could live with the founder and learn the spirit of Opus Dei from him. They could spend time with members of the Work from many different countries and acquire a personal sense of the universality of the Church and of the Work. They could study philosophy and theology in depth, and some could train for the priesthood. In a few years time, when they returned to the United States, as priests or as well-formed laymen, the benefits for the apostolate would be enormous.

Even in the short run, God blessed Muzquiz's generosity in sending people to Rome. In July 1955 he observed that "the apostolate is going much better than in other years. In fact since the first Americans left for the Roman College, we have experienced a big push. In the year since they left, there have been quite a few more vocations than in the previous five years." Msgr. Cormac Burke, an Irish priest of Opus Dei who arrived in the United States in 1955, confirms this observation:

"When I first arrived in the States, I began to realize something of his concern to send those who had joined the Work to Rome to receive formation, as he himself had, directly from St. Josemaría. In fact, his policy—which would not be normal in other times, but then showed an extraordinary depth of faith—was to send everyone he could to Rome, leaving the centers almost deprived of native members. Nevertheless (or more probably as a result of this exercise of faith) vocations continued to come in abundance in all those following years." Years later St. Josemaría commented that Father Joseph had been outstanding in grasping the importance of sending as many people as possible to Rome for formation.

IN ADDITION TO SENDING PEOPLE TO ROME, Muzquiz attached great importance to forming members in the United States. As soon as significant numbers of people joined the Work, he began to organize summer courses at which they could learn in greater depth the teaching of the Church and the spirit of Opus Dei. The first large-scale summer course, held at Woodlawn in 1956, brought together members of Opus Dei from the East Coast and the Midwest. Concentrating almost everyone in Chicago for the summer crippled the apostolate in other places, but Father Joseph was convinced the sacrifice would bear fruit both in the lives of the new members of the Work and in their apostolate.

Father Joseph's concern for the formation of the members of the Work was not limited to classes, days of recollection, and other group activities. He took time to form people one by one. Faced with shortcomings or defects, "he avoided impatience, anger, and lack of understanding, but when he observed something that needed correcting, he said it clearly, without circumlocutions, trying not to humiliate but to edify."

He gave special importance to promoting a family spirit among the members of the Work. From the beginning, Escrivá had been convinced that God wanted the members of Opus Dei to be united by strong ties, and he worked hard to give the centers of the Work the atmosphere of a close-knit Catholic family. As part of that effort, he urged the members of the Work who lived in its centers to have dinner together whenever possible and to spend some time after dinner talking about the events of the day or whatever else happened to come up. On birthdays, holidays, and feast days he urged them to make a special effort to be in the center for dinner and the get-together that followed.

Father Joseph similarly concentrated on promoting this family spirit. In the United States, individualism and a certain reserve in social dealings made it difficult for people to achieve a warm, caring tone that reflected not just formal "charity" but the affection of family members. He urged members of the Work to attach great importance to family dinner in the center, particularly on special days, even when that required a significant sacrifice. What that could mean was visible when, for instance, a prominent Spanish publisher and politician who was a member of the Work visited Washington in the early 1960s. A high-ranking State Department official who could introduce him to many important people, invited him to dinner at his home on Pentecost Sunday. The invitation was attractive professionally, and it might also have given rise to contacts that would be helpful in Opus Dei's apostolate in Washington. Nonetheless, Muzquiz suggested that the visitor decline the invitation in order to spend the feast day with the other members of the Work.

Because sanctifying work requires doing it well, down to the last detail, Father Joseph was at pains to correct even minor defects. After one class of formation, he took aside the person who had given it and said, "You said beautiful things, but you didn't get down to specifics, and the spirit of the Work is in the specifics." A young journalist who had recently joined Opus Dei was asked to edit the typescript of an article about Opus Dei that was to be published in a Catholic magazine. She did the job hurriedly and sloppily. Father Joseph, she recalls, "asked me to sit down and seated himself beside me, placing the article before me. I don't remember his exact words, but I remember that he delicately indicated that the pages were not presentable and it would be better to redo them to give it a neat and orderly appearance. It was only a few minutes, but I observed so many things: his gentleness and patience in pointing this out, taking time to do it personally, to teach me something in a memorable way instead of just sending a message; the importance he gave to detail and order; his serious demeanor without showing any trace of coldness or disdain. It struck me then that here in practice was the spirit of the Work as the founder was teaching it, and here was a priest that almost visibly resembled the Father in his way of representing him there."

In 1960 Muzquiz took a particular active role in helping a group of twenty young women who came to the United States from several countries to expand the apostalic activities of the women's branch. Meeting in Madrid with the women who were coming from Spain, he encouraged them to take advantage of their twelve-day Atlantic crossing to take special care of their interior life of prayer and sacrifice, to get to know each other better, and to have a good time. After they and a group of South Americans arrived, he served as chaplain for an orientation course held in Chicago during July and August. Carmen Gutiér-rez Ríos, who ran the course, recalled many years later with gratitude the advice she received from Muzquiz. It was, she says, "as if the Father himself was with us. We had complete confidence in him. In the first place because our Father had given him the assignment, but also because he was a very loyal son whose only concern was to carry out Opus Dei as God wanted, as the Father wanted. He led the way by example. His intelligence and wise advice were always accompanied by an amiable manner. He was always serene and gave peace to others."

9.

NEW CITIES

OPUS DEI HAD BARELY ARRIVED IN CHICAGO when Muzquiz began thinking about expanding to other cities. New York naturally caught his attention early on. In May 1950 he wrote to Escrivá: "Father, New York is very big—more inhabitants than Portugal, and almost as many as all of Canada. There is much to be done, many souls. Many of them must be good people . . . *operarii autem pauci* [but the laborers are few, Lk. 10:2]." Boston also seemed particularly attractive because of its universities and its high percentage of Catholics.

Father Joseph also focused on cities closer to Chicago. As early as March 1949, Madison, Wisconsin caught his eye. The University of Wisconsin, which at the time had some twenty thousand students, seemed a promising place for apostolate with college students. The bishop and the Catholic chaplain of the university had shown great interest in Opus Dei. And the small size of the city—although in some ways a disadvantage—meant that they would not face the problems of distance that were proving troublesome in Chicago.

Father Joseph began thinking about St. Louis after a visit to Archbishop (later Cardinal) Ritter, who was anxious to have Opus Dei begin its activities in his archdiocese. The high percentage of Catholics in St. Louis was attractive, and it struck Muzquiz as a place where the women of Opus Dei might begin a corporate apostolic activity more easily than in Chicago. In August 1951 Father William Porras, a recently ordained priest of Opus Dei, arrived in the United States. Although of Mexican origin, he was a U.S. citizen because he had been born in El Paso, Texas. He spoke excellent English, so he was able to begin working as soon as he arrived. His presence made it possible for Muzquiz to travel more extensively and to begin to implement his dreams of expansion.

In fall 1951 Muzquiz decided to make a small-scale attempt to get started in New York. Rieman and Viladas moved to the city, where they rented a small apartment at 105 Joralemon Street in Brooklyn. Rieman enrolled at St. John's University while Viladas began pursuing a Ph.D. in economics at New York University. In December, Father Joseph spent some time in New York, contacting numerous people and giving talks to groups at five or six colleges and universities. The outpost in New York would not, however, prove viable. After one semester Rieman returned to Chicago. Viladas eventually went back to Spain. In 1955, Manolo Barturen, a Spanish businessman, rented an apartment in New York, but the first Opus Dei center there would not open until 1961.

The year 1951 also witnessed a small beginning of Opus Dei's activity in Boston where both Archbishop (later Cardinal) Cushing and Msgr. Murphy, the rector of the seminary, were very supportive. In the fall a Spanish member of the Work, Santiago Polo, moved to Cambridge to begin post-graduate studies at Harvard. A few months later he was joined by Luis Garrido, another Spaniard, who began work on a doctorate in physics at Harvard.

In February 1952 Muzquiz visited Boston to see Polo and Garrido and to give talks on the sanctification of professional work at the Harvard Catholic Club, the Massachusetts Institute of Technology (MIT), and Tufts. Taking advantage of the trip, he visited Archbishop Cushing who encouraged him to press ahead in Boston. Muzquiz urged Polo to begin looking for a house. He wrote to Escrivá, "We have begun looking for a house . . . naturally with no money. But it will work."

The arrival of a third priest, Gonzalo Díaz, made it possible for Muzquiz to send Porras to Boston to care spiritually for the members there and to work on acquiring a large house. In spring 1953 they located a promising property: two attached five-story houses located near the Public Garden at 22 and 24 Marlborough Street. The buildings were being used as a boarding house.

At Father Joseph's urging the members of the Work, encouraged no doubt by the fact that he had successfully purchased Woodlawn and Kenwood in Chicago with no money, moved ahead with the purchase although they had barely a hundred dollars in the bank. They managed to get a first mortgage from a bank and a second mortgage from a young Boston lawyer to whom they had been introduced by Sal Rosenblatt, a New York lawyer whom Father Joseph had met on one of his trips. They convinced the lenders to accept a down payment of only four percent of the $51,000 purchase price, but even that was a daunting amount when they had barely a hundred dollars. A Spanish friend and Msgr. Murphy helped them with the $2,000 down payment. Although Muzquiz does not mention this in his correspondence or in his recollections, it appears that they also convinced the realtor, Ms. Mildred Baird, to donate her sales commission, as Tom Cremin had done for the purchase of Woodlawn.

The few members of the Work in the Boston area moved into the new center in December 1953. It was an enormous challenge to find residents and to convert a large, run-down boarding house into a student residence whose tone and appearance would reflect Opus Dei's spirit of doing things carefully and well as something offered to God. The problem was complicated by lack of money. Rather than clearing out both houses, they concentrated the remaining boarders—whose rent was needed to pay the mortgage—in one house while they and the handful of student residents they had been able to find occupied the other.

The 1953–54 school year and the summer of 1954 were spent largely on upgrading the buildings for their new function as Trimount House residence. The archbishop sent plumbers to remodel the bathrooms, but any member of the Work or friend who came to visit was likely to find himself pressed into service on a do-it-yourself project. Muzquiz recalls that when Father Ray Madurga, a Spanish priest who had just come to the United States, passed through on his way to Chicago, "they greeted him cordially with one hand, and with the other gave him a brush to help with the painting."

By fall 1954 the residence was up and running. Father Joseph came to Boston for the official inauguration on October 19, 1954. Archbishop Cushing attended. Several people had suggested to the Archbishop that he appoint Father Porras Catholic chaplain at Harvard. When one of the guests at the inaugural event repeated that suggestion, Cushing made a decision on the spot. Mistaking Father Joseph for Father Porras, he walked up to him and asked if he would like the job. A slightly flustered Muzquiz replied, "I think you mean that priest across the room." That day Archbishop Cushing appointed Father Porras Catholic chaplain at Harvard.

Although Muzquiz was delighted with how well the inauguration had gone, he was distressed that there had been no vocations in Boston. He returned to the same topic the next month, and again in January 1955. In a letter to Escrivá, after identifying several problems that explained the slowness of the apostolate in Boston, he added: "Pray, Father, that everything works out. I have high hopes."

In fact, Muzquiz's hopes for Boston were more than justified. Starting with the 1955–56 school year, Opus Dei's apostolate there and in nearby Cambridge grew rapidly and a number of students at both Harvard and MIT joined the work. Father Joseph played an active role in these developments. During the 1956–57 school year, for instance, he visited Boston eight times. On each visit he made time to have a get-together with the young members of the Work and to talk personally with any who wanted to meet with him. Muzquiz worked hard to relate to these young Americans. A day or two after an informal get-together in which he had teased some of them about the Red Sox and the White Sox, another Spaniard voiced his admiration at his knowledge of baseball. He confessed that he wasn't really interested in baseball and didn't know much about it, but had read the sports page to prepare for the get-together.

In the fall of 1959, a second Boston area center, eventually called Elmbrook, was opened in Cambridge, just a few minutes from Harvard Yard. Muzquiz followed these developments from a distance but with prayerful, vigilant interest. He urged the new members of the Work to look for many others so that Opus Dei could continue to expand both in the United States and in other countries. He was pleased that students from the Philippines, China, and Australia were attending formative activities organized by Opus Dei in Boston and Cambridge, and hopeful that there would be as many as twenty circles each week in and around the area, including some in Spanish for South American students, one in French, one in Italian, and possibly one in the principal Philippine language, Tagalog. At the same time, he was concerned to make sure that all new members of the Work received the in-depth doctrinal and spiritual formation they would need to live their vocation well and carry on fruitful apostolic activities.

IN THE MID-1950S MUZQUIZ WAS SENDING everyone he could to Rome, and money and experienced people were in short supply.

Things were, in the words of Father Burke, "spread extraordinarily thin." Others might have thought that Opus Dei needed to consolidate its positions in Chicago and Boston before looking to begin elsewhere. When Muzquiz sketched out his plans at the beginning of 1955, however, he envisioned starting in Madison and St. Louis in 1956 and Washington, D.C. in 1957. Things moved even more quickly than Father Joseph hoped and by the end of 1956 Opus Dei had centers in all three cities.

The new centers were opened despite an almost total lack of resources. In a letter to Escrivá, Muzquiz described the situation in Washington, D.C.: "We are dependent on the generosity of many people. They have no help for cooking or cleaning and the house is still only half set up. At times the fathers of the boys who attend activities come to paint and do repairs. A group of ladies, some of them mothers of the boys, come to give the house a thorough cleaning, polish floors, etc. Sometimes they send food when they see that the refrigerator is a little bare." Conditions in the other new centers were not much different.

Only a handful of people were available to staff the new centers and most of them were inexperienced. This required Muzquiz to travel constantly to give encouragement and guidance. Father Burke confesses that at the time he did not fully appreciate "the daring that inspired all of this; yet Father Joseph undoubtedly saw it fully, was prepared to accept the extra burdens it involved, especially for him. His attitude was always, if we rely on God he will not let us down. And so it was."

This bold expansion reflects characteristic features of Muzquiz's personality. He was by nature adventurous, and always wanted to explore new territories. He was impatient with delays, and with any tendency to just go on momentum. He had the mind of an entrepreneur, who would rather act immediately than wait until everything was in place. One person who worked closely with him as a member of Opus Dei's governing body in the United States found that at times "the goals he expected to achieve seemed unrealistically high, but the simplicity of his faith and depth of his supernatural outlook prevailed over human arguments." He was undaunted by lack of money. He did not consider the fact that a given objective far outreached their economic resources an obstacle. That was simply one of the factors to be resolved. He employed great willpower in achieving the goals he proposed, and was persevering almost to the point of stubbornness. His was an active patience that worked away with great industriousness and persistence to achieve what was fitting for the glory of God.

IN THE SPRING OF 1955, ARCHBISHOP O'BOYLE of Washington offered Opus Dei a large house in Silver Spring, Maryland, a northern suburb. In addition to selling the house at a discount, the archbishop offered to arrange a bank loan on favorable terms for two-thirds of the purchase price and to take a second mortgage at two percent for the rest. Thus, with no money down and a monthly payment of little more than $100 (at the time, the rental price of a three- or four-bedroom apartment), Opus Dei could have a large house with enough land to build a sizeable addition.

The offer was too good to turn down, even though Father Joseph could only muster one priest recently arrived from Ireland and one layman, born in the United States but raised in Colombia, to begin in Washington. They took possession of the house in early 1956. A few days later Muzquiz wrote to Escrivá, "We have a bed and a half [presumably a mattress without box spring or vice versa], three chairs, and some plates." They concentrated their efforts on preparing the oratory, and within a few months Father Joseph was able to report, "They have our Lord living in the house. Another tabernacle!" Neither financial difficulties nor the unfinished state of the house prevented the members of Opus Dei in Washington from carrying on an active apostolate. By October 1956 they were holding days of recollection practically every Sunday as well as occasional retreats.

Muzquiz promptly began thinking about using the house, called Baltimore Lodge, as an international center of formation

At Badajoz, Spain, with his mother in 1913.

A photo of Miguel Muzquiz y Fernández de la Puente, father of Fr. Joseph, taken in Havana, Cuba in 1890.

In September 1929 the young Muzquiz traveled with family members on the *Tiede* from Barcelona to Cadiz. Here he is standing behind his grandfather, Regino.

Muzquiz's father, Miguel Múzquiz, was a career army officer serving in Toledo when this picture was taken in 1913. He later resigned his commission and taught in a high school in Madrid.

Muzquiz joined the Nationalist Army in August 1936. He served for a year as a soldier and then attended officer candidate school. He is shown here in 1937 with Luis Barbeito.

Muzquiz graduated from the prestigious school of Engineering of Highways, Canals and Ports in Madrid in 1936. At that time engineers in Spain formed part of a corps which was closely connected to the Army and on special occasions wore the dress uniform in which he is depicted here.

In the early 1940s Muzquiz worked as an engineer for a Spanish railroad and in addition had his own consulting structural engineering practice. Although extremely busy with professional work, Muzquiz found time to work closely with Saint Josemaría Escrivá in spreading Opus Dei to cities outside of Madrid. Here is a portrait taken in the early 1940s.

Less than a year after arriving in Chicago with almost no money, a limited command of English and very few contacts, Muzquiz was able to acquire a large house located at 5544 S. Woodlawn Avenue on Chicago's south side near the University of Chicago. There he and the other members of the Work began a university residence which they named Woodlawn Residence. Here, the building, as it looked in the early 1950s.

Father Joseph was ordained by Archbishop Eijo y Garay in Madrid, June 25, 1944, together with Alvaro del Portillo and José María Hernández de Guernica, (standing on left) who were the first three priests ordained for Opus Dei.

Richard Rieman, the first American vocation to Opus Dei, had served as a Navy aviator during World War II. He first learned about Opus Dei during summer 1950 when he was working as technical director of the mounted units of "Frontiers of Freedom," a summer show with a cast of 150 presented on the lake front at the Chicago Fair. Shortly thereafter he joined Opus Dei.

Kenwood Residence in Chicago, the first women's center of Opus Dei.

In 1954, Muzquiz's close friend, the future Cardinal John Wright, visited him at Woodlawn Residence.

Salvador Ferigle, a physics graduate student, came from Spain with Muzquiz to begin Opus Dei in the United States. After his ordination he was known as Father Sal. Here he is in the bottom row, second from left at a lecture on Dante's Divine Comedy given at Woodlawn Residence in the early to mid 1950s by Harvard Professor Daniel Sargent (top row, third from left).

In May 1951 Father Joseph passed through Shannon Airport in Ireland where he met briefly with Cormac Burke, the first Irish member of Opus Dei. In 1955, Burke, who by that time had been ordained a priest of Opus Dei, came to the United States to help develop Opus Dei.

Patricia Lind, a cousin of Richard Rieman, was the first woman member of Opus Dei in the United States.

Father Joseph played an active role in the development of Opus Dei in Canada. He is shown in Quebec City, on Jan 27, 1979.

Rome, in June 1969, Saint Josemaría invited Father Joseph to celebrate in Rome together with Alvaro del Portillo and José María Hernández de Garnica the twenty-fifth anniversary of their ordination as the first three priests of Opus Dei. They are depicted with St. Josemaría.

Father Joseph was actively involved in beginning the activities of Opus Dei with married people. He is shown in 1976 with two of the early married members, Richard Long (foreground) and John McCormack.

Father Joseph spent the decade 1966 to 1976 as chaplain of the Pozoalbero Conference Center in southern Spain. From there he carried out an extensive apostolate with people of all social classes including many Americans stationed at the nearby Rota Naval and Air Base. He spent much of his time working with diocesan priests in the area.

Only weeks before his death, Father Joseph attended an informal get together of a thousand people with Don Alvaro del Portillo, then prelate of Opus Dei, at Hunter College in New York City.

Father Joseph celebrated his 70th birthday in 1982 at Chestnut Hill, Massachusetts, with Father Raphael Caamano, who succeeded him as vicar of Opus Dei in the U.S., and Father Sal Ferigle in the rear.

When Father Joseph came to the United States to begin Opus Dei's activities, Saint Josemaria could give him no money, but he did give him this icon of the Blessed Mother which had hung in Opus Dei's center in Burgos during the Spanish Civil War. The image was based on a painting of Jesus' mother which legend has it was painted by St. Luke.

During the final years of his life, Father Joseph was actively involved in the apostolic activities organized at Arnold Hall Conference Center south of Boston. Here he is relaxing during a summer course at the conference center.

for members of Opus Dei, with the hope that it might grow into a college. In the 1958–59 school year, the center of studies for young members began with about a dozen students from the United States and several from South and Central American countries. Muzquiz spent the thirtieth anniversary of the foundation of Opus Dei, October 2, 1958, with them. "It is a great joy," he wrote to Escrivá, "to see this group of young men beginning their studies in the interregional center. There are so many motives for gratefulness to Our Lord who has blessed us so abundantly. Last night I said so to the students during the meditation."

Father Joseph followed the development of the center of studies closely. Its chaplain recalls: "He was interested in everything: the classes of philosophy and theology, the professional activity of the students who were already working and the college or graduate studies of those who were still in the university. He also paid attention to the setup of the house and the health and rest of the students. He transmitted to us everything the Father asked him to tell us as well as the other directives he received from Rome. He oriented us on how to live the spirit of the Work and on finances. He did all of this with great refinement."

Muzquiz took a personal interest in each of the students in the center of studies, and indeed in each of the members of the Work. He was, of course, concerned about their spiritual life, but he also paid great attention to whether they got enough rest, ate adequately, and were happy. He pushed himself hard, but frequently asked others if they were tired or needed a rest. Although he was self-denying in matters of food and drink, he was visibly upset when he noticed a young member of the Work leaving the house for a summer job with a skimpy brown-bag lunch.

Father Joseph went out of his way to make get-togethers pleasant and restful. He did not sing well, but he enjoyed singing along with others simple songs like "Deep in the Heart of Texas," clapping enthusiastically at the appropriate moments.

On birthdays, he would take a popular song and write humorous new words referring to the person whose birthday it was. Plans for turning the center of studies into a college moved ahead quickly at first. In November 1958 the board of what by then was called the Maryland Institute of General Studies met for the first time. Among its members were a governor of the Federal Reserve Board, a general, a lawyer, and several businessmen. Their plan was for a four-year college with heavy emphasis on philosophy and theology and a professional orientation toward journalism. The college never really got off the ground, but the effort to start it is a tribute to Muzquiz's faith, zeal, drive, and enthusiasm.

MADISON WAS THE NEXT PLACE WHERE OPUS DEI opened a center. Starting as early as 1949, Bishop O'Connor repeatedly urged Muzquiz to begin activities there. The Catholic chaplain of the university, Father Kutchera, assured Muzquiz that it would be easy to find residents if Opus Dei opened a residence in Madison. In early summer 1955 the bishop facilitated the purchase of three houses located on a single large lot near the university campus.

As had been the case in Chicago and Boston, members of the Work did much of the work of preparing the houses for their new function as a university residence. During summer 1955 they often traveled from Chicago to spend the weekend working on the buildings. At Father Joseph's urging, one of the first tasks was to build a provisional oratory so that they could "have our Lord" with them in the house from the beginning. Friends helped solve the problem of furnishing thirty rooms. A cooperator in Chicago wrote to a friend in Madison whose husband owned a furniture factory. Another woman from Madison contacted her brother, who had friends in the furniture business, and put together a group of local women to help find used furniture.

The University of Wisconsin at the time did not have enough dormitory space for all of its students, and Madison's small size meant that there was not a great deal of off-campus housing. This made it much easier to find residents than it had been in Chicago. When the residence opened at the beginning of the 1955–56 school year, every room was taken and there was a waiting list.

The members of the Work in charge of running the residence were young, had joined Opus Dei only recently, and had little or no experience of this kind. But they naturally kept Muzquiz and the others overseeing Opus Dei's activities in the United States informed about how things were going, and Father Joseph always exhibited complete confidence in them.

MADISON WAS QUICKLY FOLLOWED BY MILWAUKEE. As early as 1954, at least one married member of the Work lived there. Archbishop Meyer, whom Muzquiz went to visit, was anxious to have Opus Dei begin in his archdiocese. During the 1954–55 school year a number of high school boys from Milwaukee made retreats in Woodlawn, and some expressed interest in possibly joining Opus Dei.

Muzquiz waxed enthusiastic in a letter to Escrivá about the beginnings of the apostolate in Milwaukee: "Things are turning out much better than we hoped. The Spirit really blows where he wills. We have had groups of boys make retreats in Chicago, but then had difficulty staying in contact with them. In Milwaukee, on the contrary, things are going full speed ahead. To give the boys a little formation, we have rented a small apartment for the summer. Some of our people from Chicago can spend weekends there or stay overnight during the week (it's only two hours by car from Chicago). . . . A wonderful thing is that the families of the boys are delighted and are giving us furniture for the apartment."

Over the next few months, a number of young men and women joined Opus Dei in Milwaukee, as did a number of married people. By early 1956 enough activity was going on there to justify seeking a house for a men's center. That summer, the archbishop offered a large two-story house that had been recently given to the archdiocese. It was located on the south side of the city, close to where many of the people who had recently joined Opus Dei or attended its activities lived.

When Father Joseph visited in January 1957, after having been absent for several months, he found the house "completely changed, with the oratory finished and some other rooms as well. It has all been done with the cooperation and donations of local people. Supernumeraries and their friends have been going in the evenings to work on the house after they finish their jobs." The new facility contributed to the rapid growth of the apostolate in Milwaukee. A number of high school students—including the author of this biography—joined Opus Dei there during 1957. The following school year, circles were organized both for high school students and college students.

As early as 1956 Milwaukee proved fertile ground for women members. That year Múzquiz informed Escrivá that more women had joined Opus Dei in Milwaukee than in the rest of the country combined. In 1958, the first women's center of Opus Dei began in an apartment. It was quickly replaced by a university residence called Petawa. It was not easy to find suitable residents or to organize the conferences and talks that would make it a vibrant university center and not merely a dormitory. One of the young women, who had come from Spain to Milwaukee, took great encouragement from talking with Muzquiz: "Not that things were easy, but he spoke with us in such a way that it seemed we had already achieved what he was asking of us."

SINCE THE TIME WHEN HE VISITED A CENTER of Opus Dei in Spain in 1951, Archbishop (later Cardinal) Ritter of St. Louis had been urging Father Joseph to open a center in his diocese. Muzquiz was attracted by the large Catholic population of the city, including many strong families and by the fact that the tradition of a strong Catholic presence went back to the city's beginnings. Unlike Boston, where Catholics were considered newcomers, in St. Louis many of the oldest and best-established families were Catholic.

The archbishop offered in 1956 to sell Opus Dei a large, well-situated house that had recently been donated to the cathedral parish. Muzquiz thanked him but declined the offer because Opus Dei had no money for the purchase. The most it could afford was a modest small apartment renting for $100 a month or less. The archbishop countered that he would buy the house from the parish and sell it to the members of the Work on favorable terms. "During the first year or two," he said, "just pay the $100 a month an apartment would cost. And since the house will be yours, anything you spend on remodeling or decoration will be yours." He also offered to help find furniture for the house. "Under these conditions," Muzquiz reported to Escrivá, "we had no choice but to accept his desires. The house is well located, can work well for us, is large and solidly built, and has a large yard that will be useful for days of recollection."

Once again, cooperators and friends stepped up to help build the oratory, furnish the house, and do the necessary remodeling. "It is a joy," Father Joseph wrote, to see how the story repeats itself in all the cities where we begin without anything."

IN THE MID-1950S BILL DUFFY, WHO HAD ATTENDED Opus Dei activities in Chicago, enrolled in the University of Notre Dame. For the next four years, members of the Work traveled from Chicago to South Bend to hold meditations, circles, and other activities for Bill and his friends, usually in the homes of Opus Dei cooperators. Bill graduated in 1958, but his place was taken by John Gueguen, a political science instructor, Bernie Browne, a graduate student in international relations, and Hilary Mahaney, an undergraduate from Maine and pitcher on Notre Dame's baseball team.

By spring 1960 there was enough activity to justify looking for a house that could serve as a center. Mahaney found a promising house on Notre Dame Avenue close to the campus. As usual the problem was lack of money, but Gueguen endorsed his paycheck to the seller as a down payment, and eventually they managed to find financing for the rest of the purchase price. On June 25, 1960, they moved into the house, and on June 28 Mass was celebrated for the first time in what would be called

Windmoor Study Center, the last Opus Dei center to be opened during Father Joseph's first period in the United States.

DURING THE MID-1950S, IN ADDITION TO promoting Opus Dei's geographic expansion, Muzquiz was also widening the scope of its activities to include married people and priests. From the beginning of Opus Dei, Escrivá had envisioned it as comprising people God called to holiness in married life as well as those whom He called to celibacy. It was not possible, however, to admit married members, called supernumeraries, until the Holy See gave Opus Dei its definitive approval in 1950. Thus, before coming to the United States, Father Joseph had no experience of organizing the activities of married members. During the first few years in the United States, he concentrated on looking for people who could receive a call to apostolic celibacy in Opus Dei and would be in a position to dedicate themselves to helping it grow and expand in the country.

In March 1952, he began to look for married people who could understand and live the spirit of Opus Dei as supernumerary members. A little more than a year later, in July 1953, the first married American asked to be admitted to Opus Dei. By summer 1954 there were half a dozen supernumeraries in the Chicago area and a sprinkling in Wisconsin, Ohio, Indiana, Massachusetts, and New Jersey. After that the number of married members grew rapidly.

Another area of Opus Dei's activity with which Muzquiz had no prior experience was its apostolate with diocesan priests. They, too, could benefit from practicing Opus Dei's spirit of seeking sanctity in and through daily work and activities, in their case their priestly ministry. From a canonical point of view, however, it was not easy to see how they could fit into Opus Dei. Not until after Muzquiz moved to the United States did Escrivá discover a way for them to belong to Opus Dei while remaining priests of their own dioceses, fully dedicated to the pastoral tasks their bishop had given them.

Around 1956 Muzquiz began to spend time on apostolate with diocesan priests. He showed special concern for them, and soon had many priest friends. When traveling he would gladly go out of his way to meet a priest who had expressed interest in Opus Dei or been recommended to him by a mutual friend. Soon priests in a number of dioceses joined Opus Dei with their bishops' blessing. Said one of them: "Every time I met him, I could feel his special joy. He looked at you and he sparkled. He had an inner happiness. Ultimately, I think that holiness is an inner joy you have in your relationship with God. That is how I always saw Father Joseph."

BESIDES OVERSEEING OPUS DEI'S GROWTH in the United States, Muzquiz was actively involved in the expansion of Opus Dei to Canada and Japan. Jacques Bonneville, the first Canadian member of Opus Dei, joined in 1955 while studying for a doctorate in engineering at MIT. That same year, he and his family returned to Quebec. Perhaps in part because Bonneville was there, Escrivá originally thought of Quebec as the best place for beginning Opus Dei's apostolic activities in Canada. Muzquiz went there to speak with Archbishop Roy. He suggested to Escrivá that one way of getting started would be for a French-speaking priest to make trips from Boston.

In fact, however, Opus Dei's first Canadian center would be in Montreal, not Quebec. In March 1957, after a visit from Cardinal Léger of Montreal, Escrivá decided that Montreal would be a better place to begin. He sent Muzquiz there to talk with the Cardinal and do the spade work. In characteristic fashion, Father Joseph made this changed plan his own. He did not minimize the complications of beginning in a place with a mixed French/English population, but he stressed the advantages of starting in a larger city with a more open environment and where there were already several people who knew Opus Dei and would be willing to help.

Shortly thereafter Escrivá invited a young Spanish priest, Father Martín, to go to Montreal to begin Opus Dei in Canada.

"You don't have anything to worry about," he told him. "Father Joseph will have thought of everything." Muzquiz drove Father Martín from Boston to Montreal, took him to a residence for priests, and the same day got back into the car to return to Chicago. A few weeks later, Father Joseph appeared again in Montreal, this time on his way from Chicago to Boston.

Toward the end of the summer, Cardinal Léger offered to give Opus Dei the use of a house that could serve as a small student residence. Muzquiz liked the house and considered it a gift of God. "If you are ever tempted by discouragement," he told Martín, "just go out and take a good look at the house. Walk around it, giving thanks to God, and you'll recover right away."

Escrivá named Muzquiz his delegate in Canada. In that capacity, he made frequent trips to visit the people of the Work and to encourage them in their incipient apostolic endeavors. A young Spanish engineer who was the first lay member of the Work in Canada recalls with gratitude those visits. He was in a difficult situation. After six months of looking, the only job he had been able to find was as a draftsman. As the only lay member of the Work in Montreal, he was named the director of the student residence, although he had no experience in running a residence and great difficulty communicating with the few residents since he could barely speak French or English, although he could read both. He found Father Joseph's visits a stimulus in every sense:

> His affection, the faith with which he spoke to us, the piety with which he celebrated holy Mass, the peace and security he inspired, his apostolic zeal (it was incredible how many people he knew), all of this was a godsend that gave us renewed enthusiasm and vigor.
>
> I cannot reproduce specific words of his, but I recall the get-togethers we had with him in a 12' x 18' room with only one window in a half-basement. That room was the office of the regional commission, the bedroom of the head of Opus Dei in Canada (who slept on a sofa bed), and the living room where

we could have get-togethers apart from the residents. The lack of means was evident, but it was no obstacle to having a good time being with him and hearing news of our Father and of the apostolate in other countries.

One of the early women members of the Work in Canada echoes those sentiments. "We really felt the Father's presence when Father Joseph transmitted to us his words, his desires, his indications for the apostolate, his affection and his confidence in us. Father Joseph was an instrument of unity who kept us close to the Father. He could do this not only because of his natural qualities but because he was himself so closely united with the Father and because he had such a sense of urgency about extending Opus Dei in Canada."

MUZQUIZ ALSO PLAYED A KEY ROLE in the early history of Opus Dei's apostolate in Japan. When he visited Rome in the fall of 1957, Escrivá told him that the bishop of Osaka, who was in Rome at the time, was interested in having Opus Dei work with college students in his diocese. Because Japan was so far away and so different from the other countries in which Opus Dei was active, Escrivá did not want to make a commitment without further information. He asked Father Joseph to go see the bishop and make arrangements for an exploratory trip.

When Muzquiz visited the bishop at his residence in Rome, he urged him to come to Japan in mid-April when the cherry blossoms would be at their peak. "I don't think you care much about cherry blossoms," Escrivá commented when Muzquiz reported on his visit, "but go whenever the bishop wants." Father Joseph arrived in Tokyo on April 19, 1958, after a flight in which he prayed, as Escrivá had suggested, to Our Lady Star of the Sea for Opus Dei's future apostolate in Japan. After celebrating Mass in the parish of a supernumerary member of the Work who had moved to Japan from Chicago two years earlier, he wrote to Escrivá and then left for Osaka.

In Osaka Father Joseph stayed with the bishop and had his first experience of Japanese hospitality. Decades before sushi became popular in Europe and America, he considered eating raw fish "the *non plus ultra* of Japanization." He drew the line at soaking in hot water in which the bishop had already soaked (after bathing with a wash cloth and running water). He limited himself to dipping a finger in the tub so that when the bishop asked him if the temperature was all right he could truthfully answer "it was perfect."

Escrivá had asked Muzquiz to kiss in his name the earth where so many martyrs had given their lives for Christ. Muzquiz at first thought he could do so anywhere in the country. When the bishop told him that there had been no martyrs in Osaka, Father Joseph decided to visit Nagasaki. He arrived there on May 1. In Nagasaki he made his May pilgrimage and celebrated Mass at an altar beneath a picture of Our Lady that a French missionary had brought in the nineteenth century.

During his stay in Japan, Father Joseph talked with the bishops of Hiroshima, Fukuoka, and Nagasaki and their collaborators, as well as with missionaries from a large number of countries. He concluded that it would be hard for Opus Dei to get started in Japan, both because of the difficulty of the language and because the Japanese viewed Christianity as part of a foreign culture which they were reluctant to accept. He was confident, however, that Opus Dei's work in Japan would eventually be effective, especially because of the high esteem in which the Japanese held science and culture.

For part of the return trip from Nagasaki to Osaka, Muzquiz took a ship through the Interior Sea. He was pleased to have the opportunity to pray to Our Lady Star of the Sea. While sailing among the many islands, he thought of the many people who had crossed the seas to bring Christ to Japan and of the members of the Work who would go there with hopes for the conversion and sanctification of many.

When he returned to the United States he brought with him a number of snapshots which he passed around in get-togethers with members of the Work. Paul Deck, who was in one of those get-togethers observes that the pictures "were not impressive in their content nor quality, but the joy with which he presented them manifested a great enthusiasm—based on supernatural hope and optimism—for the future apostolate in the country."

Muzquiz made several more brief trips to Japan to help get Opus Dei's apostolate started there. Naturally much of the apostolate was with non-Catholics. Under the canon law of the time, it would have been possible to baptize in an Opus Dei center those who wished to embrace the faith. But Father Joseph's respect and affection for the diocesan and parish structure of the Church moved him to encourage the members of the Work to direct people for their final instruction in the faith and their baptism to the parish to which they would eventually belong. This sensitivity to the importance of the local church contributed greatly to helping Opus Dei put down roots in Japan.

IN 1961 ESCRIVÁ CALLED MUZQUIZ to Rome to work Opus Dei's international governing body, the General Council. When he left the United States centers existed in Boston, Washington, St. Louis, Milwaukee, Madison, Wisconsin, and South Bend, Indiana. From the four people who accompanied Muzquiz on the train to Chicago, Opus Dei had grown to several hundred members in the United States. Half a dozen young American professional men had been ordained as priests of Opus Dei, and a sizeable number were studying philosophy and theology in Rome. Many of them would be ordained and others would return to help direct and expand Opus Dei's activities in the United States, or would go to other countries to start Opus Dei there. In addition, Opus Dei was getting started in both Canada and Japan, thanks in large part to Father Joseph's efforts.

PART III

ROME AND SWITZERLAND

—— 1961–1966 ——

~ 10.

ROME

At the end of September 1961, Muzquiz took up his new position on the General Council. His duties involved working with Escrivá and the women responsible for directing Opus Dei's apostolic activities with women throughout the world.

Working on the General Council, like serving on any of the regional or local governing bodies of Opus Dei, was a collaborative, collegial affair. Escrivá insisted on having several people involved in every decision as a way of improving the quality of decision-making by overcoming the innate human tendency to dominate others. Most of the work was done in writing. Meetings were few and brief. Muzquiz had long been accustomed to this way of working, but previously it had occupied a fraction of his time, which was otherwise taken up with preaching, hearing confessions, giving spiritual direction, and traveling to cities where Opus Dei had centers.

Father Joseph had greatly enjoyed transmitting the spirit of Opus Dei to people through direct personal contact, and loved traveling for this purpose. In Rome, days and even weeks could go by in which he hardly ventured out of the complex of buildings where he lived and worked, rarely seeing anyone except other members of Opus Dei. His days were taken up with paperwork. Escrivá reminded him and the other members of the General Council that they needed to see souls behind the papers and realize that their work made a direct contribution to bringing people closer to God. Convinced that this was true, Father Joseph offered his work for the people who would be directly affected by the projects he was working on, for friends and acquaintances, and for people in contact with Opus Dei's apostolates whom he had heard about but had not met. He cannot, however, have found this as immediately gratifying as dealing personally with people and seeing them grow in the love of God.

On the other hand, he greatly enjoyed living and working with Escrivá. He and the other members of the General Council living in Rome saw him regularly for questions related to work. Escrivá also preached meditations to them and directed the circle or class of Christian formation they attended each week. After both lunch and dinner, they had informal get-togethers with him. Sometimes in those get-togethers Escrivá talked with them about the spirit of Opus Dei and about events in the life of the Church, particularly the Second Vatican Council (1962–1965). Frequently they told jokes, sang, and just enjoyed one another's company while talking about the events of the day, anecdotes they had heard about Opus Dei's work throughout the world, and a wide range of other topics.

In 1962 Escrivá gave Muzquiz a small gold pocket watch, which he himself had used for many years. It had an unusual rectangular design, with a case which, when closed, completely covered the face. Opening and closing the case wound the watch. Muzquiz would use and treasure the watch for the rest of his life; many people noticed that it reminded him to pray for Escrivá.

AMONG THE PROJECTS FATHER JOSEPH WORKED on in Rome was the development of a new home for the Roman College of Holy

Mary, the international center of formation for women members, which had been established in the 1950s. The new site, located in Castelgandolfo in a villa donated by the Holy See to Opus Dei, would make possible a larger and more ambitious program. An important element of the new program was a university-level International Center of Pedagogy. Students of the Roman College of Holy Mary interested in teaching careers would be able to obtain college degrees in education there while studying philosophy and theology and receiving formation in the spirit of Opus Dei. Muzquiz was actively involved in developing the curriculum for this new project.

Even in a setting where hard work for love of God was the norm, Father Joseph's seemingly endless capacity for work stood out. He worked very quickly, and his co-workers found his style and work habits distinctly "American." Escrivá and the people who lived with him had to take pains to get him to rest and to take care of his health, since he didn't complain even when suffering migraine headaches. One person who worked closely with him says that he would not even have known that he had migraines, had someone else not told him.

In 1964 he came down with hepatitis and was confined to bed. Escrivá realized that he was temperamentally incapable of just lying there passing the time. He suggested that he study the history of the Church in Asia. Someone got him a collection of journals from a library that specialized in that subject. Muzquiz read his way through them systematically, taking one off the pile on one side of his bed and transferring it when he finished to a pile on the other side.

MUZQUIZ TOOK ADVANTAGE OF THE PRESENCE of Australian bishops in Rome for the Second Vatican Council to lay the groundwork for Opus Dei's apostolate in that country. The papal nuncio to Australia, whom he had met in Japan, put him in touch with Cardinal Gilroy of Sydney. Father Joseph took the Cardinal and several other Australian bishops to visit a university residence run by Opus Dei in Rome. Gilroy was much impressed by its atmosphere and invited Opus Dei to start one like it in Sydney. Shortly thereafter, in 1963, the first members of Opus Dei went there to begin work. Among them were several Americans.

WHEN MUZQUIZ WAS APPOINTED TO THE General Council, plans were being made in the United States for a conference center in the Boston area and for a large international men's residence for Harvard and MIT students. In 1963 a property that seemed suitable for a conference center was found in Chestnut Hill, a suburb of Boston. Opposition from the neighbors, however, forced the abandonment of that project, much to the disappointment of those who had invested a great deal of time and energy in it. During a visit to Boston, Father Joseph told them they "should not feel bad about the loss. Simply, God had prepared for us something much better. We had to look harder, because that property would have been small very soon, and we had to have a vision for the future." Not content with encouraging the members of the Work to continue looking for a site for a conference center and to pray harder, Muzquiz took advantage of the few days he spent in Boston to contact realtors himself. He asked them to look for a suitable site and also for a large new house in Boston for the women's branch.

By early spring 1964, a realtor had found a private school located on a large piece of land in Pembroke, Massachusetts, about forty-five minutes south of Boston. It had ample room for future construction and a number of buildings that could be used in the meantime. The property seemed ideal, but two things were still needed: money and the approval of Cardinal Cushing. One of the people involved in the purchase recalls that Father Joseph solved the first problem in characteristic fashion. "He conducted the negotiations with the owner so swiftly, and with such faith, that he was able to walk away from the table with exactly what he had wanted: the entire property for a fraction of the price."

Until a short time before, it would have seemed that the blessing of the Cardinal could be taken for granted. An enthusiastic supporter from the beginning of Opus Dei's activities in the archdiocese, he had repeatedly shown his affection with public statements and financial contributions. But at the time of the negotiations to buy the property in Pembroke (eventually to be called Arnold Hall), serious misunderstandings had arisen in connection with the project for an international student residence. They threatened to derail the conference center as well.

At first the project of an international residence progressed rapidly. The Cardinal wrote a letter in support. A board of distinguished civic leaders was formed, and a one-acre lot only a few blocks from Harvard was acquired. Unfortunately, the bitter opposition of the priest who had succeeded Father Porras as Catholic chaplain at Harvard turned the Cardinal, quite ill at the time, against the residence.

Escrivá sent Muzquiz to Boston to try to calm the storm. Father Joseph met with many people, including the chaplain. The architect for the project, who was present at the lunch Muzquiz arranged with the chaplain, was struck by Father Joseph's "amazing self-control." "I was impressed with how serene, understanding, and pleasant Father Joseph was in such a strained and almost belligerent circumstance. He was constantly friendly and never argumentative during the entire luncheon...even though he had, in justice, every right to be."

Muzquiz did not change the chaplain's mind, but in a meeting with Cardinal Cushing he did succeed in assuaging his concerns. During this meeting, Father Joseph was consistently positive, never saying anything negative against the priest or anyone else. The project for the residence would eventually be abandoned, but Muzquiz obtained the Cardinal's blessing for Arnold Hall Conference Center in Pembroke.

~ II.

SWITZERLAND

OPUS DEI'S ACTIVITIES IN SWITZERLAND began in 1956, but in 1963 they were still struggling. The women of Opus Dei had not begun working in the country, and the men had a single center, Fluntern, a small student residence in Zurich. Responsibility for activities in Switzerland still rested with Opus Dei's Regional Commission in Milan because the volume of activities in Switzerland did not justify creating an independent Regional Commission for that country. Escrivá hoped Muzquiz's vibrant faith, drive, and enthusiasm might produce a breakthrough.

Escrivá was aware of the contrast between the highly regimented character of Swiss society and Muzquiz's restless, free-wheeling personality and rapid-fire style. Wanting him to see the virtues of the country before asking him to direct Opus Dei's apostolate there, he sent him in late 1963 to visit and report back. As Muzquiz was leaving, Escrivá spoke with him enthusiastically about Switzerland's importance as an international crossroads and about the "colossal" work that could be done there to contribute to Opus Dei's activities in many countries.

In July 1964 Muzquiz left Rome to head Opus Dei's activites in Switzerland. Immediately upon arrival he threw himself into adapting to the country. From his years in Rome he spoke some Italian, but his French and German were limited. Nonetheless, he quickly began to hear confessions and to preach in all three languages. German was especially challenging, but with careful preparation he soon began to preach half-hour meditations in simple but correct German.

Hans Freitag, at the time a member of the newly created governing body of Opus Dei in Switzerland, recalls that Muzquiz immediately set a "new, accelerated, pace in all our work." He was an example of hard work and good use of time. Along with fulfilling his duties as head of Opus Dei in Switzerland and carrying on an intense personal apostolate, he found time to earn a doctorate in canon law.

Building on his experiences in the United States, he suggested beginning courses for high school students on study methods and introductions to the professions. The courses proved popular and brought many students into contact with Opus Dei. He remodeled the building that housed the student residence creating three separate zones. The student residence occupied the ground floor and the upper floors. Offices and living quarters for the Regional Commission were located in a semi-basement. What had been a dirt-floored cellar became a large activities area with a study room. Much to the surprise of many, Father Joseph rapidly raised the necessary funds from local businesses.

SHORTLY AFTER MUZQUIZ'S ARRIVAL, THE FIRST two women of Opus Dei came to Switzerland. Once things were a bit settled, they would be joined by women from several countries. Although at first there were only the two of them, Muzquiz came to their house every day to say Mass on an improvised altar. In frequent meditations preached to these women, he insisted repeatedly on the same themes: love of God and confidence in Him, doing things as the Father wanted them done, apostolate. Although both he and they were native Spanish speakers and it was slow work for him to prepare meditations in German, almost immediately he began to preach to them in German to help them learn the language and adapt.

He began a series of classes for them on Escrivá's "Instruction on Winning New Vocations." The classes initially were held in the kitchen, because that was the only place where there were a table and chairs. At first, while they had no phone, Father Joseph made a point of dropping by frequently with another priest in case they had questions or things they wanted to talk with him about. Carla Arregui recalls his "humble attitude and his great simplicity." She had joined Opus Dei only two years earlier and had never occupied a position of government, but Muzquiz asked her opinion about what needed doing and listened with great interest and attention.

One day, shortly before he was due to arrive to say Mass, Arregui noticed that they had no hosts. Since they still didn't have a phone, she hurried out to meet him on the way and ask him to bring hosts. Just as she arrived at a point from which thirty or forty steep stairs led down the hill, she saw Muzquiz beginning to climb up. When he saw her at the top, he gathered up his cassock and began running up the steps, panting and shouting, "What happened? What is wrong?" She excused herself for having startled him, but he cut her off, saying, "Not at all. Don't fail to let me know if you need something, anything at all."

When Muzquiz learned of an opening in the University School of Translators and Interpreters, he suggested that Arregui apply. She felt that she lacked the necessary qualifications, but Father Joseph, without heeding her protests, looked at her affectionately and repeated softly, "Don't worry, don't worry about anything, because this is the will of God. . . . We will pray that everything go well." Encouraged by his confidence, she applied for and won the position, which she held for many years.

The women of Opus Dei had no sooner gotten started in Zurich than Muzquiz began urging them to make trips to Geneva. When they had been in the country a year and had held one German summer course for foreign students, he suggested they look for a house in Fribourg so that the next summer they could have a German course in Zurich and a French course in Fribourg. Money was tight, and one of the women observes that they managed only "thanks to his encouragement. Humanly it didn't make sense, but it worked."

The father of one of the young women did not understand her decision to join Opus Dei, much less her moving from Spain to Switzerland. When Muzquiz traveled to Spain in 1966, he made a point of visiting him at his office in Bilbao. The visit was a complete success. Her parents wrote her saying that had they met Father Joseph earlier they would have been spared many worries; her father added that he had had the impression of talking with a saint.

MUZQUIZ QUICKLY SET HIS SIGHTS ON GENEVA as a target for Opus Dei's expansion, but the focus shifted to Fribourg when Pope Paul VI told Escrivá in a private audience that he hoped Opus Dei would soon begin apostolic activities in that city where an important Catholic university was located.

Soon the men of Opus Dei purchased a house in Fribourg for a student residence. Muzquiz was eager to open the residence and found it hard to accept the slow pace of construction in Switzerland. Accustomed to the more expeditious regime of the United States, he found the detailed requirements of Swiss regulations and the frequent inspections frustrating to the point that he suffered stomachaches brought on by tension. He joined the other members of the Work in painting and getting the house ready, but they needed money for furnishings and for the more specialized work they could not do themselves. Each morning Muzquiz set out to find people who could contribute the necessary money.

One day on the stairway he met a tenant, a retired professor, upset at having to move out. Those present feared the scene might turn ugly, but Father Joseph listened patiently and affectionately while the man poured out his complaints. Soon he revealed the real source of his unhappiness: his twenty-year-old son had left home and disappeared. Muzquiz's sympathetic interest won him over, and when eventually he moved he left some furniture for the future residence.

Escrivá had pointed out to Muzquiz the importance of Switzerland as a world crossroads, and he quickly began to seek out foreigners who might understand Opus Dei. Besides hearing confessions in French, German, and Italian, he found a place for confessions in English in a nearby parish. In that way he met a number of people who began to attend Opus Dei activities, among them Zoltan Szabo, a Hungarian violinist who is today a member of Opus Dei in the United States.

In spring 1966 Muzquiz was only fifty-four-years old, but he had been working extremely hard for many years and was aging rapidly. Escrivá decided it would be good for him to return to Spain and take a less stressful position. He wrote, "I tell you out of affection for you that you're going to return to Spain. That way you'll be near your parents." As he did throughout his life, Muzquiz cheerfully accepted this new assignment.

PART IV

SPAIN

—— 1966–1976 ——

～ 12.

CHAPLAIN OF POZOALBERO
CONFERENCE CENTER

Muzquiz's first assignment in Spain was as chaplain of an Opus Dei center in Cádiz, a relatively small town on the Atlantic coast in the far south, about fifty miles from Seville and only a short distance from a large American naval base at Rota. After about a year in Cádiz, he was named chaplain of a conference center called Pozoalbero, which was used for nearby retreats, classes of religious formation, and workshops.

From 1966 to 1976 Father Joseph spent most of the week in Pozoalbero, but at least once a week he returned to Cádiz to spend time with other members of the Work in the center there, attend means of formation, and receive personal spiritual direction. The young director of the center was apprehensive about giving spiritual direction to Father Joseph, who was already a member of the Work when he was born. But the experience, he recalls, was "marvelous." "His simplicity, docility, affection, and common and supernatural sense were so evident that after talking with him I was edified and thanked God for giving me the opportunity to deal so intimately with such a holy soul."

Muzquiz adapted quickly and apparently effortlessly to his new situation. Despite having spent most of his adult life in positions of authority in Opus Dei, he demanded no special attention, tending rather to pass unnoticed as just one more priest. In get-togethers, talks, and meditations, he was happy to talk about Escrivá, the early history of the Work, and its expansion to other countries. Rarely, though, did he speak of his own role and activities.

In this regard Muzquiz was a magnificent example of the aspect of Opus Dei's spirit and practice that Escrivá described in a 1974 letter. "Young persons and those not so young have gone from one place to another with the greatest naturalness, or have persevered faithfully in the same spot without growing tired. When needed they have completely changed their work, leaving behind what they were doing and undertaking a different task of greater apostolic interest. . . . They have joyfully accepted hiding and disappearing, letting others move past them: going up and coming down."

POZOALBERO HAD FACILITIES FOR RETREATS, workshops, and other activities for adults, along with separate areas for activities for young people. In an independent part of the compound there was a center for the administration, the women who formed the permanent staff of the conference center and were responsible for running it and taking care of meal service and housekeeping.

Father Joseph's principal duties were to provide spiritual care for the women who worked in the administration and to support their personal apostolate with women who lived in the area by giving meditations and classes and hearing confessions. The task of preaching the retreats held at Pozoalbero and ministering to the people who came there for workshops and other activities normally fell to priests who accompanied each group, although Father Joseph often volunteered to help hear confessions and give personal spiritual direction.

These assigned duties might seen minimal, resembling quiet semi-retirement in the country. In fact, Father Joseph's ten years in Pozoalbero were a whirlwind of activity. He threw himself with extraordinary generosity into the pastoral care of the women who worked in the administration and the support of their apostolate with local people. In addition, he heard confessions and gave spiritual direction in nearby parishes and Opus Dei centers, frequently visited a hundred parish priests scattered around towns and villages in the area, organized retreats, days of recollection, and workshops for priests, and carried on a vigorous personal apostolate with many other people including Americans stationed at the naval base at Rota.

"Call me whenever you need me," he repeatedly told the director of the administration. Every evening he called to ask her how the house and the people working there were doing. His optimism and cheerfulness proved invaluable support to a young woman who took over as director of the administration when she was twenty-six and had belonged to Opus Dei for only a couple of years: "When things got to me—in large part because of my immaturity—talking with him gave me the strength and light I needed to take them on with serenity and joy. . . . I never saw him without a pleasant smile. No matter how serious a problem might be, he never gave it much importance. Even the most difficult situations didn't make him lose his hopeful and determined view of things. I would dare to say that he was 'incapable' of worrying or of taking a negative approach to anyone or anything."

Pozoalbero was designed to accommodate about forty adults for a retreat. On one occasion there was a mix-up that saw some 150 women showing up at the same time. The women in charge of the administration were so flustered by this avalanche that all they could think to do was send everyone home. Muzquiz was undaunted. "We can take care of it. We'll put extra chairs in the oratory and tables in the dining room. I'm sure they'll all fit. Let's thank God that so many have come. Don't let anyone leave."

As he had done in Switzerland, Father Joseph preached half-hour meditations more frequently than the standard one per week. When he received a letter from Escrivá, he immediately wanted to share its spiritual content with others, and any feast day or anniversary of an important event in Opus Dei's history was an occasion to preach. On important anniversaries he also offered to tell the people working in the administration stories of the early days of Opus Dei, anecdotes about Escrivá or the origin of points in his book *The Way*. But not everything was about spiritual matters. Muzquiz had a good eye for amusing details and knew what would interest people. Returning to Pozoalbero after a lengthy trip to Africa, he told the women whose duties included laundry how in Africa men did the laundry in the river, using long sticks to beat the clothes against rocks.

The physical labor of running a large conference center at a time when modern appliances were still unknown in southern Spain was often overwhelming. The women in the administration understandably felt they had little time for recreation or for other apostolic activities, beyond running a small catechism class and supplementary education program for girls from the immediate area and giving formation to members of Opus Dei who lived nearby. On days when the conference center was unoccupied, they often took advantage of the break to clean more thoroughly, but Muzquiz would tell them that the house was already clean and would urge them to take the opportunity to get out and enjoy themselves.

He was especially interested in helping them extend their apostolate to more people. That seemed impossible for lack of time, but he helped them devise a work plan that gave all the women at least two free afternoons weekly—time to visit friends or run apostolic activities. He urged them to keep a master list of all the women and girls they had met or even heard about, ranging from the wives of owners of vast rural estates to Gypsy girls living in shacks. Frequently he helped them review the list and make plans for working with each person. No matter how tired they were or how concerned with the problems of running the center, he managed to rekindle their enthusiasm for the apostolate.

Not content with simply urging these women to reach out to more people, Father Joseph generously supported their projects. Each week he spent hours in the confessional ministering to local girls who could hardly read. He treated them with fatherly patience, even when several would crowd into the confessional at the same time. One extremely hot summer day he was scheduled to give a brief talk to some barely literate girls who lived in shacks nearby. Finding himself delayed, he phoned to say he would be a few minutes late but would be there soon, and the girls should not leave.

DURING THE DECADE MUZQUIZ SPENT AT POZOALBERO, southern Spain was a highly stratified society, with great extremes of wealth and poverty. With only slight exaggeration, he described it as in some respects still feudal, with little communication among the social classes. But his work embraced people of all social classes and economic conditions, from poor, virtually illiterate workers in a nearby sugar beet mill to owners of the great estates that dominated the area, from high school girls in Jerez to American naval officers stationed nearby.

Muzquiz wrote to Escrivá with evident enthusiasm about the efforts underway among hairdressers, bartenders, and a woman whose whole family had to work from before sunrise to late in the evening harvesting olives because her husband had lost his regular job. One person tells of him visiting a family that lived in a hovel and entering their shack "with the joy of someone entering a palace."

He was equally at home with the rich and famous. On several occasions, he helped organize retreats especially for bullfighters, adapting the schedule and the talks to their mentality. The elderly owner of one of the finest sherry-producing vineyards accepted Father Joseph's invitation to a retreat after many years of turning down invitations from others. He explained to a member of the Work, "What your brothers couldn't achieve with all their wordiness, Don Jose Luis achieved with his humility."

Some members of the traditional local aristocracy led relaxed, not to say indolent, lives. Making friends with them, Father Joseph helped them put away their self-indulgent lifestyle. He told Escrivá about the diverse mix of people helping prepare a new women's center in Jerez: from ladies with a large staff of servants to some of the people who worked for them. "Occasionally," he added, "they have ended up working together in the center, something that never happens in their homes for the simple reason that at home these ladies never work at all."

Muzquiz frequently visited the nearby American naval and air base at Rota where he made friends with a wide range of people. The attendance at an annual open house that he organized at Pozoalbero for Americans from Rota was so large the police had to control the flow of traffic. On several occasions, Protestant chaplains came with their wives. Although few of the women who worked in the administration spoke English, he convinced them that they were fully capable of entertaining the American guests. One of them recalls that "he got those of us who knew a little English to talk with the guests as best we could while the others accompanied them with a smile."

Father Joseph organized and preached days of recollection and even an occasional retreat in English. Among those attending were the commander of U.S. nuclear submarines in the Mediterranean, an Anglican chaplain, the head Catholic chaplain at Rota, and a Catholic chaplain from an American base in Morocco. A number of the Americans whom Muzquiz met at Rota became members of Opus Dei when they returned to the States.

A large part of his time was spent hearing confessions and giving spiritual direction. He was effective as a confessor and spiritual director because he combined deep faith, supernatural outlook, and love of God with humility and simplicity. It was not so much what he said as who he was that moved people. As one person observed, "In a way that is hard to define, he had an extraordinary capacity to communicate a sense of God, and even of God's presence, to everyone he met."

A priest to whom he gave spiritual direction recalls that when he first met Father Joseph he was "confused and in conflict" due to difficulties arising from the tasks assigned him by his bishop. "From the first time we met, he could see that I needed somebody to give me support. So he singled me out. He would invite me, 'Let's take a walk.' As we walked, we talked. He would let me unload a lot of my frustrations and angry feelings, and then give me direction, so that by the time we came back, I was already feeling a lot more supported and at peace with things. The direction he gave me was very positive."

Father Joseph's approach as confessor and spiritual director was based on confidence in God's fatherly care along with common sense and serenity. With regard to the spirit of penance, for instance, he did not discourage people from rigorous fasts or other extraordinary mortifications when it appeared that was what the Holy Spirit was asking of them, but he would remind them that first and most important was to live the spirit of mortification in everyday events: spending time straightening out a closet, writing to family members, fixing something around the house.

In asking people to live a spirit of sacrifice in small things, Muzquiz was asking them to do as he did. At breakfast he habitually ate toast with nothing on it, no butter or jam. Before dinner on big feast days, he would have a drink to join in the spirit of the event, but such a small quantity that the glass contained mostly ice. While apparently having a drink like everyone else, he was really just shaking ice around in a glass. One sweltering hot summer afternoon as they were returning home from a tiring day, a person with him said he was dying of thirst, and Muzquiz immediately proposed that they have a Coke. After a few minutes of chatting, the other person had downed his Coke, but Muzquiz had barely sipped his.

Despite his insistence on the importance of little things, Muzquiz did not hesitate to demand major sacrifices when necessary. A member of the Work who had committed himself to celibacy frequently visited some relatives who lived near his office. He mentioned to Muzquiz that he often found himself talking in depth with a young woman, not a relative, living with them. After getting a few more details, Father Joseph advised him not to visit those relatives in the next year. "I could have fallen in love with her," the man recalls. "His advice . . . did great good for my interior life and helped me gain freedom of spirit." Another person who made a retreat with Muzquiz during a critical period of her life found that following his demanding advice restored her hope and peace. It was effective, she believes, because it was "the result of his dedication to God."

Often it was Muzquiz's good humor that helped people. One day a young man told him he was deeply concerned about the future. "What will happen to me in twenty-five years?" he asked somewhat melodramatically. Muzquiz looked at him over the top of his glasses, jotted something in his notebook, and answered: "I can tell you one thing for certain." "What is that?" the young man asked with interest. Father Joseph then assured him that some absurd possibility would not be part of his destiny, and they both laughed. That was the end of his worries about the future.

At times his example was sufficient by itself to resolve previously intractable problems. A person who could not seem to overcome certain serious difficulties found the way to resolve them during a retreat. He did not speak privately with Muzquiz on that occasion, but just observing his simplicity and how he lived out the spirit of the Work moved him to begin again.

ALL PRIESTS NEED SUPPORT, ENCOURAGEMENT, and guidance in their spiritual life. Priests who, like most of those in the area around Pozoalbero, live isolated in small towns and villages may have a special need for help to avoid falling prey to loneliness and discouragement. Supporting their brother priests is a specific apostolate of the priests of Opus Dei, and Escrivá encouraged

Muzquiz to dedicate himself especially to it, "loving them, dealing with them with affection, teaching them to serve the Church with refinement."

Whenever Father Joseph passed through a town or village in his travels, he stopped briefly to visit the parish priest. Finding the priest in, he would chat with him for a few minutes. If the priest was out, he wrote a short note and went on. Not content with visiting those whose parishes were on his way, he would systematically visit priests in all the towns and villages of the area, no matter how small and out of the way and no matter how bad the roads. Many were grateful for his visits. "They want to talk and many times to open their hearts," Muzquiz told Escrivá. "One told me, 'I didn't sleep all night I had so many worries. Fortunately you came by so I had someone to talk about them with.'"

During the years Muzquiz lived in Pozoalbero, priests needed special help to assimilate the teaching of the Second Vatican Council and to distinguish between what the Council taught and the aberrations some justified as 'the spirit of the Council.' Muzquiz tried to befriend all the priests he met, even those whom some other priests dismissed as "revolutionaries." In most cases, he realized, it would be counterproductive to engage in theological debates, but "at least I can reach out to them with concern and affection."

Muzquiz organized frequent talks, classes, days of recollection, and other means of spiritual and intellectual formation for priests. When Pozoalbero's schedule of other activities permitted, he held one- or two-day workshops where someone gave a talk about a topic in the news. Because the facilities at Pozoalbero often were not available and because it was hard for many priests to get there, Muzquiz also organized activities in small roadside restaurants or in homes. In his eyes, as important as the content of the talks and classes he arranged was the opportunity for the priests to spend a few hours or days together, becoming better acquainted and establishing bonds of friendship, fraternity, and mutual support.

All this required that Father Joseph travel a great deal over bad roads to reach remote villages. He drove a Seat 600, the cheapest car on the market, tinny, harsh-riding, and so small that it was hard to get in or out. With a twenty-one horsepower engine it was badly underpowered. It had no air conditioning, although midday temperatures during the summer often hit 105 degrees. Muzquiz frequently returned to Pozoalbero exhausted after a long day of driving over poor roads in the heat, but the doorkeeper noticed that no matter how tired he was he entered the house smiling.

Thanks to Father Joseph's spirit of sacrifice, a large number of priests began little by little to attend workshops, days of recollection, retreats, and informal lunches and dinners. In the course of a few weeks at the end of 1970, Muzquiz talked to more than a hundred diocesan priests.

Some of the priests Muzquiz dealt with eventually joined the Priestly Society of the Holy Cross, a part of Opus Dei that provides diocesan priests guidance and support in seeking sanctity by carrying out generously their priestly ministry and being closely united to their bishop. Muzquiz worked especially hard to promote a sense of fraternity among those priests. At Christmas he invited them for dinner and a celebration at Pozoalbero. He prepared gifts for everyone—usually of no great value but thoughtfully chosen—accompanied by humorous verses that he wrote and adorned with drawings.

Thanks to Muzquiz's encouragement, support, and personal dedication, the apostolic activities conducted from Pozoalbero expanded greatly during his decade there. Many people of all social classes came closer to God, and a number discovered that God was calling them to Opus Dei.

～ 13.

THE DEATH OF
JOSEMARÍA ESCRIVÁ

WHILE MUZQUIZ LIVED AT POZOALBERO, ESCRIVÁ was actively seeking the right place for Opus Dei within the Church's legal structures. He asked his sons and daughters throughout the world to pray for this intention, and Father Joseph responded with characteristic generosity. He wrote to Escrivá: "I want to be very united to your intention, Father, but at times it seems that I don't pray as I should. For that reason, I've taught myself to get many other people to pray, those I go out to see and those who come to Pozoalbero. I hope that in this way our Lord will hear the clamor we are raising."

Muzquiz wrote frequently to Escrivá telling him about his apostolic activities. Every now and then he took advantage of the opportunity to say that he was happy where he was, but ready to do whatever might be asked of him. "Father, I want to help you in everything you want. Even as I age, I want my heart to be younger every day." "I'm happy here and there's lots to do, but I would be equally happy anywhere you may want, even to begin a new apostolate."

In 1968, Opus Dei celebrated its fortieth anniversary. When someone suggested that Escrivá might spend the anniversary in Pozoalbero, he at first showed little interest, but when he was reminded that Muzquiz was there, he immediately accepted the suggestion. Father Joseph was delighted to be able to spend the anniversary with Escrivá. A year later, Escrivá invited Muzquiz and José María Hernández de Garnica to Rome to celebrate the twenty-fifth anniversary of their ordinations together with Alvaro Del Portillo. When Father Joseph uncovered the chalice at Mass on the morning of the anniversary he was moved to discover that it was the chalice given him for his ordination by his engineering classmates. Shortly after his ordination, at Escrivá's suggestion he had left the chalice in an Opus Dei center in Spain for use by the center's priests, and he had not seen it for years. Escrivá had gone to the trouble of having it brought to Rome for the occasion.

During a two-month catechetical trip to Spain in 1972, Escrivá spent the week of November 6–13 in Pozoalbero. Muzquiz was overjoyed to see him surrounded by thousands of members of the Work and their friends, who came for informal get-togethers. He was especially pleased that among the priests of the area attending a get-together for more than two hundred priests of the Priestly Society of the Holy Cross was an eighty-year-old priest whom he had met a few years before.

JOSEMARÍA ESCRIVÁ DIED SUDDENLY OF A HEART ATTACK on June 26, 1975. That day Father Joseph was hearing confessions in the town of Sanlúcar. When the news came, the people waiting for confession expected him to leave immediately, but when one of them asked him, "What are we going to do now?" he responded, "You're going to go to confession, and I'm going to hear your confession." That, he added, was what the Father would want, since he had always insisted on sticking to the schedule for confessions. To another person who asked much the same question, he answered, "Stay happy and keep working, as if nothing had happened. Don Alvaro [Del Portillo, the Secretary General of

Opus Dei] will tell us what to do." At the same time, he was asking himself, "How can it be . . . when we most needed him . . . it's not possible." But he quickly corrected himself: "Fine. It's nothing to worry about. We don't know why, but God has permitted it."

Upon returning to Pozoalbero, he went to the oratory with the other members of the Work to pray a liturgical prayer for the deceased. He was deeply affected, but insisted on the need to be serene and tranquil. He slept little that night and spent the time largely in prayer. The next day, at the same time as Escrivá's funeral was celebrated in Rome, he celebrated a funeral Mass in the oratory of the administration at Pozoalbero. Most of those present were weeping, but Father Joseph celebrated with peace and serenity and advised them that Escrivá would want them to be serene and carry on with their work.

Convinced that Escrivá would be a powerful intercessor, especially for things related to Opus Dei's work, Muzquiz immediately began to pray to him. Shortly after his death, a younger priest of Opus Dei told Father Joseph about an undertaking of his that had not turned out well. Muzquiz asked if he had entrusted the matter to Escrivá's intercession. When the priest said no, Muzquiz commented, "Since our Father went to heaven, I entrust everything to him, and he does it."

IN SEPTEMBER 1975, MUZQUIZ TOOK PART IN THE congress at which Alvaro Del Portillo was elected Escrivá's successor as head of Opus Dei. Immediately after Del Portillo's election, Muzquiz, like the other electors, went to kneel and kiss his hand. As he did so, he said, "Father, I'm ready to do whatever is needed." Del Portillo pulled him to his feet and gave him a warm embrace while calling him "my son, Jose Luis." From that moment, Muzquiz addressed Del Portillo as "Father," the title by which the head of Opus Dei is usually addressed. Despite their long and intimate friendship, Father Joseph from then on used the respectful "*usted*" form rather than the familiar "*tú*" he had used till then in speaking with Del Portillo or writing to him.

When he returned to Spain, Muzquiz was eager to tell other members of the Work about the electoral congress and about his conversations with Del Portillo. One recalls that he spoke about Del Portillo with the enthusiasm of "a little boy." She adds, "It was a great lesson in humility and in filiation to see him speak with such veneration and affection about the Father, considering that he was the same age and that along with him he was one of the first priests of the Work."

Shortly after being elected Escrivá's successor, Del Portillo decided to ask bishops all over the world to consider writing to the Holy See to request the opening of Escrivá's canonization cause — the formal process of study and investigation that could lead to his being declared a saint. Knowing Muzquiz's love for travel to bring the spirit of Opus Dei to people in new places, Del Portillo asked him to visit bishops in Sierra Leone, Liberia, Ivory Coast, Ghana, and Upper Volta (today, Burkina Faso) and to report on the possibilities for Opus Dei's future expansion in those countries. Accompanied by Juan Masiá, Father Joseph spent January 1976 visiting bishops in the region. Their longest stay was in Abidjan, Ivory Coast, where the conference of bishops of French-speaking West Africa was meeting. Later Muzquiz liked to recall how part of the trip had been by canoe.

A member of Opus Dei who worked in the administration of Pozoalbero, a native of Guinea, had lost contact with her family during a period of civil unrest in the country and did not know if her parents were still alive. Muzquiz made a side trip to Guinea and located them. When she tried to thank him for having gone so far out of his way, he replied that since the Work is a family, it's natural that one person's concerns should concern the rest.

IN 1976, DEL PORTILLO ASKED FATHER FLORENCIO Sánchez Bella, the head of Opus Dei in Spain, to sound out Muzquiz, who was then in his mid-sixties and once again in good health, about returning to the United States to direct activities there. Sánchez Bella asked Muzquiz to come to Madrid for a talk, without specifying what he had in mind. Before leaving Pozoalbero, Father Joseph asked people to pray that he might be ready to do whatever was asked of him. When Sánchez Bella told him the Father wanted him to consider returning to the United States and let him know how he felt about the prospect, Father Joseph replied that he didn't need to think about it. If the Father wanted him to go, he would go.

Muzquiz immediately wrote Del Portillo recalling the occasion when Escrivá asked him to go to the United States for the first time. "Now I will go with the same enthusiasm—I would even say with the same youth—as then. But now I will also go with the help from heaven of our Father. And since I know that you will pray a lot for the apostolate there, I'm sure that will be another great aid." To another member of the Work he said he was happy to return to the United States since it underlined the fact that in Opus Dei age alone was not a reason for retirement.

In a long meeting before his departure for America, Del Portillo told Muzquiz his appointment was to be an interim one. The long-range plan was for Rafael Caamaño, a Spanish Naval Academy graduate who had been deeply involved in the government of Opus Dei both in Spain and in the United States, to head Opus Dei in the United States. Caamaño was, however, still a layman, and it would take a few years for him to be ordained and then, as a priest, to acquire knowledge and experience regarding the activities of Opus Dei's women's branch. Muzquiz left for the United States in October 1976, taking with him only one small suitcase.

PART V

UNITED STATES

—— 1976–1983 ——

~14.

HEAD OF OPUS DEI IN
THE UNITED STATES (1976–1980)

MUZQUIZ SPENT THE NEXT FOUR YEARS AS HEAD of Opus Dei in the United States. As in the 1950s, his fundamental approach was to ask himself "What would our Father do in this situation?" Concerned not with his own opinion but with finding the best way of doing things, he was anxious to get the input of others. He was so refined in the way he presented his ideas and so naturally respectful of the views of others that they found it easy to say what they thought. Even in minor matters, he was open about projects he was working on and eager for suggestions for improving something he had done or written.

He listened to the opinions of others with great respect and readily accepted them, unless there was a reason that required the opposite. This was especially true with the women's branch. A woman member of the board that directs Opus Dei's activities with women in the United States observed: "Father Joseph did not tell us what to do. His way of governing was—as St. Josemaría taught us—based totally on trust. He respected down to the last detail St. Josemaría's wish that the women govern themselves. He only intervened directly when it was a matter of spirit, which we might not be following faithfully by inadvertence. In those cases he was clear and firm."

Muzquiz led with decision and firmness, but "disappearing." His style of leadership reflected a completely supernatural outlook—a kind of consciousness that this had to be the work of God or it would be nothing at all. When a local director relatively new to the Work expressed discouragement with the way things were going and concern about his own lack of qualifications, Father Joseph reassured him: "Don't worry. God is the one who runs Opus Dei."

Muzquiz scrupulously avoided micromanagement. His attitude has been summed up as "get it done, pass it on to the person who has to handle it next, step aside, and let it run." He would follow issues, but with a style of working that was quick and efficient. He made the directors of Opus Dei realize clearly "what our responsibilities were, what needed to be done, in general terms. Or he would inform us of a possibility, suggesting that we may want to think about it. And then with admirable patience, he waited for us to come up with the right decisions or measures."

Father Joseph aspired to govern "with a mother's heart and a father's arm." By example and advice he taught other directors to deal with one another and everyone else with refined charity. On one occasion he asked a director to write an informal note to an architect about a project he was working on. It was late in the evening and the person was tired. When he showed Muzquiz the dry, perfunctory note he'd written, Muzquiz told him the tone was wrong for something intended for a brother in the Work and asked him to rewrite it in a warmer, more affectionate style.

Though he was a hard-driving man, he always seemed ready to change tack on a moment's notice at the slightest suggestion of Don Alvaro Del Portillo. He was always extremely attentive to the mind and will of the General Council of Opus Dei. When mail arrived from Rome, he would drop whatever he was doing and turn to the mail. If there was anything he was being asked to do, he would turn to it immediately.

He saw directives from Rome not as impositions but as helps in carrying out the apostolate. His attitude is reflected in a letter he wrote to Del Portillo when a visitor came from Rome with news about things there and instructions for the United States: "We greatly appreciated the news he brought us as well as the notes about how to promote the apostolate with young people and give formation to those who recently joined the Work. Pray, Father, that those of us on the Commission may know how to put them into practice, that I may find the right way to transmit this apostolic drive, and that from the Commission we may help to move the centers forward."

Father Joseph's principal concern was seeking holiness and contributing to the personal sanctity and fidelity of the members. He asked Del Portillo "to pray for the fidelity—the personal sanctity—of all your daughters and sons in this region. It's the only thing I'm really concerned about. If we grow in holiness and self-giving, we will grow in everything else, and the whole apostolate will grow."

If the members of the Work were to grow in holiness and expand their activities, formation was a vital necessity. "Really our only problem—which I hope will grow—is the formation of new members, and the formation of those who have to form them. All of the people are good, but many of the directors of the centers have little experience and we have to follow them closely and affectionately because they are 'young.' Pray, Father, that we may fight this 'battle of formation' as our Father called it with generosity and energy, because here it is of primordial importance."

Besides organizing classes, conferences, etc., Muzquiz took advantage of every opportunity to form in the spirit of Opus Dei the people with whom he lived and worked as well as other members he encountered from time to time. A close collaborator says: "Father Joseph was always forming people. He was always trying to teach us something. But not in a way that was uncomfortable. It was enjoyable. It was interesting. He had good stories that would open up our eyes about the spirit of the Work through the things our Father did with him."

MUZQUIZ FREQUENTLY ENCOURAGED MEMBERS of the Work to expand their horizons and to look for more people who could respond to God's call to serve Him and the Church in Opus Dei. In this he met with great success. In the first quarter of 1977, more people asked to be admitted to Opus Dei than in all of the previous year. By spring of 1978, he was hoping that by the end of the year the number of numeraries in the region would be twice what it had been at the beginning of 1977. He believed Opus Dei was beginning to take off in the United States like "a plane that has just left the airport. It still has a long way to go, but the important thing is that the motors run well."

Although things were looking up, Father Joseph was fully aware of how much remained to be done. As the thirtieth anniversary of his first arrival in the United States approached, he wrote to Del Portillo: "It is a motive for thanksgiving to God, and at the same time to examine our consciences and see that things are going slowly—they have gone slowly, and they still are going slowly. We are just a few drops of water in the ocean that is this great country. I try, Father, to see things with serenity and supernatural outlook and to encourage my brothers and sisters as much as I can."

Growth in numbers brought with it a need for more space. Muzquiz saw Escrivá's intercession at work in the finding of a new temporary home for the center of formation for young male members in New York as well as a new center for professional men in Washington D.C., and a campus for The Heights School on the outskirts of Washington.

Centers of the women's branch multiplied in similar fashion. In 1977, Oakcrest, a school for girls in Washington that a year earlier had begun in rented quarters, purchased a more adequate site. Simultaneously, a center was opened nearby for apostolic activities with students and their mothers. That same year, the women of Opus Dei opened a center of studies in Newton, Massachusetts, a center near The Willows Academy in Chicago, and Lexington Institute, the nucleus of what would eventually become Lexington College in Chicago.

This rapid expansion was made possible by Father Joseph's faith and daring. When people worried about paying for it all, he often responded simply, "God is rich." "When you heard that said without a shadow of hesitation," a director of Opus Dei's activities with women in the United States recalls, "signing mortgage papers was easy."

WHEN MUZQUIZ RETURNED TO THE UNITED STATES, the Regional Commission of Opus Dei had its offices and living quarters in an apartment building in Manhattan. The location was good, but the space was too small and the building was poorly maintained. For some time they had been looking for a large building in Manhattan to serve as permanent home for the national offices and a center of formation for young members.

About a year after Muzquiz returned, it seemed that they had found an ideal solution in midtown Manhattan, but they were outbid at the auction. Muzquiz accepted the setback with characteristic supernatural outlook. He told Del Portillo: "I'm sure that in the end we'll find something better.

Further searches in Manhattan proved fruitless, and Muzquiz reluctantly decided to look in the suburbs. After they found a large house in one of the northern suburbs of New York, Muzquiz wrote Del Portillo: "We have prayed . . . a great deal for a long time—years—to find a new place, so undoubtedly this is the best solution for now."

AS HEAD OF OPUS DEI IN THE UNITED STATES, Father Joseph was careful to keep the bishops informed about Opus Dei's activities. Shortly after returning to the United States, he went to the semiannual meeting of the bishops' conference in Washington,

D.C. During the meeting he prayed frequently to the bishops' guardian angels, then credited them with being able in the course of a few days to meet briefly with some sixty bishops. As he had done with priests in the south of Spain, he made a point of greeting bishops of every tendency, not just those he thought would be especially sympathetic to Opus Dei.

Muzquiz had no opportunity to meet John Paul II during the papal visit to the United States in 1979, but he worked to make it a success. He urged Opus Dei's centers to organize three-day prayer vigils and to mobilize the members of the Work, its cooperators, and everyone in touch with it to make the Pope's welcome warm and enthusiastic. He followed the trip with great interest and wrote detailed letters to Del Portillo about encounters between members of the Work and John Paul II.

THOSE WHO WORKED WITH MUZQUIZ or had occasion to deal with him on a regular basis were impressed that he focused his entire personality upon the spiritual life and apostolate. While traveling by car with other members of the Regional Commission, "he talked mostly about the history of the Work, about our Father, about how to organize and promote the apostolate. . . . His whole focus was on the important things." His attitude was "we don't have time to waste. There are a lot of things to do, places to get to, people to see, issues to resolve. So let's talk about that." He was anxious to hear about the personal apostolic activities of members of the Work so as to encourage them. It was evident from his questions and level of interest that he was earnestly praying for their friends to respond to God's vocational graces. It seemed that he never forgot a name.

As he did throughout his life, during his second term as head of Opus Dei in the United States Muzquiz manifested a special love for Our Lady. This was evident when Del Portillo declared a Marian Year in 1978 in thanksgiving for Opus Dei's fiftieth anniversary. When he decided to extend it for another year, Muzquiz wrote to thank him: "I recall what our Father often said about athletes who fail to reach the goal on the first attempt and have to try again. Since my results have not been what our Lord wanted, this second Marian Year gives me another opportunity." Father Joseph encouraged the construction of a small shrine of Our Lady on the grounds of Arnold Hall, and blessed it when completed. In later years, as chaplain of Arnold Hall, he greatly enjoyed bringing local children to the shrine for a May crowning.

During summer 1980, while the Regional Commission settling into its new headquarters in suburban New York and remodeling was in full swing, Father Joseph came down with a kidney infection complicated by prostate problems that confined him to bed. Michael Barrett, who was principally responsible for taking care of him and bringing him his meals, found it "edifying to see how he accepted this illness and the whole situation with an optimistic spirit. He offered it up for particular intentions. He would say let's offer this up for so and so (usually someone he hoped God might call to Opus Dei), or for some other intention. He maintained a supernatural outlook even when he was in pain."

When the doctor told him he would need surgery in the near future, he began praying to Escrivá that the operation not be necessary. He wrote Del Portillo: "I don't mind the operation—other than the waste of time it entails—but if it is for the glory of God and of our Father that it not be necessary, that would be wonderful."

In the days immediately following the surgery, he could not celebrate Mass, although he could receive communion. One day he asked someone who was with him to hand him the watch Escrivá had given him years earlier. Rather than checking the time, he held the watch as he made his thanksgiving as a reminder of Escrivá and to ask his help in receiving Communion well. On the feast of Our Lady of Sorrows he was able to offer Mass in his room for the first time since the operation. "I was sure," he commented, "that Our Lady would make it possible for me to say Mass since it's the anniversary of the first time

Mass was said and the Blessed Sacrament reserved in a center of the Work in the United States."

Muzquiz' strong interior life was the foundation of his optimism and hope. A person who knew him well was impressed that he "never saw Father Joseph show signs of discouragement. He never lamented without hope the sad conditions of modern culture. He was keenly aware of individual and social sin against God and His Church, but he was so prayerful that they didn't cause him anxiety or despair."

His interior life also made him understanding and supportive of others in their weaknesses, whether great or small. At a workshop for priests of Opus Dei, "he intervened to make some very enthusiastic remarks about how we could help souls in those moments in which they opened up to Jesus and to us. He insisted on how important it was to help people repent if they were not living some point in accordance with the clear teaching of the Church. He urged us to get them to pray, to face the issue before God, to ask Our Lord for the courage and strength to change their attitude. It was a matter of getting them to want to live in the grace of God, of giving them some practical advice, warming them up to sincere repentance, and then giving them absolution, inviting them to return and speak more in depth about the issue."

His understanding manifested itself in small matters as well. During a workshop in Arnold Hall, people laughed when he mentioned that a woman had written to say that St. Josemaría had cured her sick dog. Rather than joining the laughter, he commented gently that God knows how to reach people's hearts, and in this case curing the dog was a good start.

To an outside observer, it might seem that all this came naturally to him. But Father Joseph worked at growing in prayer and sacrifice and at living the spirit of Opus Dei better each day. As he had done since joining Opus Dei and would keep doing until the end of his life, he struggled during this period to put ever greater love into the norms of piety and the plan of life he had learned from Escrivá, making the Mass the center of his day, dedicating a half-hour every morning and afternoon to mental prayer, saying the Rosary, and striving to be aware of God's presence throughout the day. He focused especially on the subject of his particular examination of conscience, and this was usually the principal topic he talked about each week in receiving spiritual direction.

The person who gave him spiritual direction during the final years of his life observed that Muzquiz took to heart Escrivá's advice to use the particular examination as a sword for doing battle in the interior life. "I could suggest to him something that might be useful for him to struggle on and he would accept it with perfect docility no matter how small a matter it might be. Part of that docility, it seems to me, came from the fact that he would put himself into his particular exam with such vigor that he could get huge mileage out of whatever I suggested."

FATHER JOSEPH WAS AWARE FROM THE BEGINNING that his appointment as head of Opus Dei in the United States was temporary. As soon as his designated successor, Father Rafael Caamaño, arrived, Muzquiz started bringing him up to speed. He wrote to Del Portillo: "Since Rafa arrived, I've tried to inform him about everything. I am praying a lot—as I have been doing since I came here four years ago—that the person who succeeds me will really move all the apostolates forward. If I remain in this country, I will continue trying to help him and everyone else with the same affection I received from our Father and from you when I came to this country in 1949. Although I will turn sixty-eight in a few weeks, I feel young on the outside, and especially on the inside, with a desire to transmit to my brothers and sisters supernatural optimism and zeal for winning new vocations."

Caamaño told Muzquiz that Del Portillo wanted him to say where he would like to go when he stepped down. Muzquiz wrote to Del Portillo:

You know that I have never expressed a preference for going to one country or another, and that I would be happy in Spain, in the Ivory Coast which I visited in 1976, or wherever I'm needed. But since Rafa [Caamaño] said you wanted me to write you, I have thought about it in prayer, asking our Father's aid. I think the best thing would be to remain in the United States. This is not only because of the affection I have for this country, and especially for the members of the Work. The principal reason is that—although the people are good—I think they need to go deeper into the spirit and traditions of our family. I think that without the responsibilities of governing, I could continue to help as an older brother to transmit the marvelous family spirit that we have received from our Father.

Del Portillo replied: "After so many years of work carried out with supernatural vision and apostolic desire, I want to thank you with my whole heart—also in the name of our Father—for the spirit of sacrifice that you have shown so abundantly during all this time in carrying out the Work. I think I am fulfilling an obligation of justice in providing you a little well-merited rest, changing your occupation. I said that to you when we talked before I named you the new head of the Work in the United States. . . . Your successor has asked me to leave you in that region where you worked with all your heart from the beginning, and where you are so justly loved."

~ 15.

CHAPLAIN IN BOSTON

MUZQUIZ SPENT THE FINAL YEARS OF HIS LIFE as chaplain of the center where he lived in Chestnut Hill, a suburb of Boston, as well as of three women's centers in the Boston area. The lifting of the burden of heading Opus Dei in the United States seems to have been a relief for him. "Being in charge of the Region took years off Father Joseph's life," one person commented, "while being relieved from that job put years back onto it. It was amazing to see how different he was before and after. . . . Father Joseph was a new man. He was a young man again."

On his desk in Chestnut Hill he placed a small leather frame with two pictures. One was a photograph of a painting of Our Lady in the main oratory of Opus Dei's headquarters in Rome, reminding him to raise his heart frequently to Mary in the course of his work. The other was of Escrivá. At the bottom of the second picture he put a small strip of paper cut from a larger sheet on which Escrivá had written, "Jose Luis, talk to me." It helps me, he told Del Portillo, to "have recourse with confidence and affection to his intercession for all of his intentions and for your intentions, Father."

As he had told Del Portillo, Father Joseph saw his role largely as fostering a family spirit among the members of Opus Dei in the United States. He focused on this theme in meditations and talks because he was convinced that the American members of the Work had big hearts but needed to be encouraged to show them. He led by example, showing his own affection and concern for others in many small ways. His conversation centered on the person he was talking with, not on himself. When a member of the Work from Chicago expressed concern about an elderly aunt living alone fifty miles from Boston, Muzquiz found someone to look in on her regularly. A woman who worked at Arnold Hall recalls that when he handed in laundry to be washed, "you could see that he was thinking about the people who would do it and making their work easier and more pleasant." Whenever he stayed at Arnold Hall just a few nights with the intention of returning soon, he took the trouble upon leaving to write a note saying there was no need to change the sheets.

Father Michael Manz who lived with him in Chestnut Hill, says that despite his experience, his past responsibilities, and his seniority in Opus Dei, he behaved "as just one more person and never gave the least impression of requiring special recognition or treatment." At a public Mass celebrated by a bishop on the anniversary of Escrivá's death in one of the parishes near Muzquiz's home in Chestnut Hill, people were surprised to see him sitting with families in the church's cry room. An organizer of a gathering for priests held in New York just a few weeks before Muzquiz's death was astonished when, just before it began, Father Joseph asked with complete naturalness if he could find him a seat. "I was amazed at the humility of this simple request from the priest who had not only started Opus Dei in the United States but was one of the first three priests of Opus Dei. I had assumed that a seat had already been reserved for him."

He did not like to be served or to cause a fuss. Because of his age and stooped posture, people usually offered to carry things for him, but whenever he could he would politely decline. Far from expecting or requiring people to defer to him, he often deferred to those who were much younger. When, for instance, he and another priest were both at Arnold Hall, he did not consider himself in charge and left it up to the other to decide the schedule and other details of their stay.

He was happy to make himself available for whatever needed doing and took great interest in the apostolic activities of people he worked with. Since the centers where he exercised his priestly ministry were widely separated, he had to spend much time getting from one to the other, especially in the final years of his life when he could no longer drive and relied on public transportation. His ability to serve these centers, one person observed, "can only be explained by his extraordinary dedication and spirit of service, his sense of order, and above all his zeal for souls." Nor did he merely fulfill his duties. Each group he served, "felt Father Joseph was 'their' priest. He communicated a real interest and involvement in all places." On his frequent visits to Arnold Hall to celebrate Mass, preach, and hear confessions, he would call the director before leaving to make sure he had not missed anyone who'd asked to see him or simply dropped by asking to see a priest.

Father Joseph was always ready to tell people about Escrivá and the history of Opus Dei. During his several weeks in Madrid testifying in Escrivá's canonization cause, he participated in ninety get-togethers in which he talked about Escrivá. Back in the States, he put together a slide show to illustrate the beginnings of Opus Dei in Chicago, and if people didn't ask to see it he often volunteered to show it. One day he was scheduled to show the slides in Cambridge, Massachusetts, but a heavy snowstorm struck the Boston area forcing schools and businesses to close. Everyone assumed Muzquiz would not want to venture out in such weather, but when the director in Cambridge called him to set a new date, he was preparing to leave to catch the subway and then walk half a mile from the subway stop to Elmbrook. The visit was, of course, rescheduled.

As he had done in southern Spain, Muzquiz took a special interest in meeting and getting to know diocesan priests in the Boston area. At the invitation of Auxiliary Bishop Daniel Hart, he and Father Manz organized a monthly day of recollection for priests in Brockton, a town just south of Boston. He also made it a practice to visit priests, dropping in without an appointment because his purpose wasn't to have a formal meeting but simply to say hello and let the priest know about some upcoming activity or event that might interest him or his parishioners. While usually keeping these casual visits short so as not to interrupt the priest's work, he was prepared to spend more time if circumstances required. As the months went by, he became friends with priests throughout the Boston area, some of whom eventually joined the Priestly Society of the Holy Cross.

IN THE FINAL YEARS OF HIS LIFE, MUZQUIZ continued his efforts to grow in interior life and love of God. He did not add new practices of piety to the plan of life he'd learned upon joining Opus Dei but sought instead to put ever-greater love and attention into carrying out each of the norms that comprise it. Although his priestly work at Arnold Hall, located about an hour from Chestnut Hill, often required him to be away from the center, he went out of his way to receive spiritual direction every week, to attend the weekly circle, and to receive the Sacrament of Penance. If it was impossible to get back to Chestnut Hill for the circle, he would ask another priest who happened to be at the conference center to give a circle there, even though he was the only person in attendance. After forty years in Opus Dei he rarely heard anything in a circle that he hadn't heard many times before, but he was anxious to attend because it was an opportunity to examine his conscience and formulate resolutions about responding with greater love and care to some of the points raised.

Those years were marked by an especially deep love for the Blessed Mother. Some afternoons, when his schedule at Arnold

Hall allowed, Muzquiz would make a Marian pilgrimage in the woods. This involved tacking a picture of Our Lady to a tree and then walking through the woods praying the fifteen decades of the Rosary, planning his route to take him back to the picture and then back to the house. He habitually prayed the Rosary slowly and attentively, so that those observing got "the distinct impression that he was lost in conversation with Mary." Praying the Rosary with him led people to feel intimately united to our Lord. A priest says simply that praying the Rosary with him was "a lesson in piety." Father Joseph prayed fervently, not only for people he was personally in touch with, but for many others who he knew were taking part in Opus Dei's activities. Once he asked Father Manz to tell him who had attended the latest meeting of a circle that had only recently begun, and when the two priests ran into each other on the street a few weeks later, he asked how one of the people was getting along.

FATHER JOSEPH'S DEEP COMMITMENT AND LOVE of God made a lasting impact on people. An engineer living in the Boston area recalls the first time Father Joseph told him that he was called to holiness: "I questioned this for weeks, time and time again. Me called to sainthood? Wasn't that preposterous for a man with a worldly and sinful past? It took me months to accept Father Muzquiz's advice. At the same time, I slowly became aware that he was truly a perfect example of a living saint: extremely humble and affable, a great spiritual counselor . . . For fifteen years Father Muzquiz's call to sainthood has rung every day in my ears."

A close friend recalls:

> During a particularly difficult time in my life, Father Joseph came to visit our home. . . . The house was a mess, the kids were running around, and I was an emotional wreck. Father Joseph was unfazed. When I apologized he smiled sweetly and said, 'Don't worry about it. Think of it as confirming me in

my vocation.'" I laughed and felt immediately at ease. Before he left, he blessed our home and family. I felt restored and I think it was then that I first thought of Father Joseph as a living antidepressant. I would come to him with what I thought were impossible problems and he would help me overcome them. Once when I faced a particularly severe problem, he told me to pray to Mary and Joseph and assured me that he would do the same. . . . He took the time to know me and my wife and I trusted his advice completely.

In June 1983, just two weeks before Muzquiz's death, Msgr. Alvaro Del Portillo passed through New York on his way back to Rome from a pilgrimage to Our Lady of Guadalupe in Mexico. Father Joseph was anxious to be with him as much as possible and took careful note of what he said. In a get-together with a small number of people, Del Portillo noticed Muzquiz taking notes and asked him what he was writing. "Beautiful things, Father. Beautiful things," he responded. "You're right," Del Portillo replied. "You know them as well as I do, but they are beautiful things, because I'm not saying anything that I didn't hear from our Father."

On Sunday, June 5, 1983, the feast of Corpus Christi, almost a thousand American members of Opus Dei and their friends met with Del Portillo in an auditorium in New York. Someone who was there called the occasion "a kind of harvest feast of the many years of Father Joseph's labors in the United States." As he hugged Muzquiz, Del Portillo said, "You have to thank God and feel great joy seeing that the Work has put down deep roots in the United States."

～16.

WORKING FOR
GOD TILL THE END

A PHYSICAL EXAMINATION IN JUNE 1983 showed Muzquiz's blood pressure to be well controlled by medication and his health excellent for someone his age. On June 19, Father Manz picked him up at the Chestnut Hill center and they drove to Arnold Hall where Father Joseph was to teach classes and provide priestly services to women attending a three-week course, while Manz would be chaplain for a course for high school girls. That evening Manz asked Muzquiz for an anecdote to use in the meditation he would preach the next morning. Muzquiz offered him the notes he had prepared for the meditation he himself would preach. He also invited Manz to look through a file containing notes he'd made from meditation outlines St. Josemaría had provided when preparing Opus Dei's first three priests for ordination. This was not an isolated gesture. Years earlier Muzquiz had offered to give him that same file to a priest recently arrived from Spain who was nervous about having to preach his first retreat in English.

The next morning breakfast was late. Manz thought he should skip breakfast so as not to be late for a class he was scheduled to teach, but Muzquiz phoned the director and explained that Manz would be delayed a few minutes. When the food finally arrived, he insisted that Manz eat a full breakfast, even though he was having only toast and a cup of coffee. When it was time for his own class, he left Manz to finish breakfast and went off to teach.

During the class, Father Joseph began to feel ill. Wishing not to alarm the students, he said he had to return to his room to make a phone call. One of the students, a physician, was concerned by his appearance and asked Manz to look in on him in the priest's apartment. Manz was surprised to find him lying on the couch. He was even more surprised when Muzquiz did not dismiss the suggestion of going to see his physician, Dr. Thomas Bowman, a married member of Opus Dei whose office wasn't far from Arnold Hall. In a few minutes, however, Muzquiz started feeling better. Phoning the Chestnut Hill center to say he'd changed his plans and would not be coming for the weekly circle, he returned to class. But soon he felt worse. He ended class, and he asked Manz to take him to the doctor's office. When they arrived around 12:30, Dr. Bowman recounts, "he was as always calm and cheerful. First he asked how my wife and our new baby were. Then he related the events of the preceding few hours. As he spoke, he was having pain under his arms, which he minimized by saying 'It's nothing; it will go away.'"

An electrocardiogram showed that Muzquiz was having a massive heart attack. His condition was so serious compared with his minor complaints that the doctor repeated the electrocardiogram before concluding that he should go by ambulance to the nearest hospital, in Plymouth. Bowman told him the next forty-eight hours would be critical, and that in the best of cases he would have to rest for a month. Muzquiz remained calm, and even tried to get the doctor to say he could preach meditations while recuperating. Would he be able to sit up? "Yes." Would he be able to talk? "Yes." But then Dr. Bowman, who knew Muzquiz well, caught his drift and told him — to Muzquiz's chagrin — that he wouldn't be able to preach. Though only a few hours from death, Manz comments, "He was not thinking of dying. He was not even thinking of resting, but of serving God and souls in his priestly ministry."

Dr. Bowman went to make a phone call, and Muzquiz and Manz were left alone together. "He started saying how grateful he was to God that this had not happened when he was alone somewhere on the highway, that I had been able to accompany him, that the doctor had been able to see him right away, that this was the first time in his life he had had any serious illness, that he did not feel intense pain or discomfort . . . In short, all he could do was to think of reasons to be grateful to God for his loving care."

On the way to the hospital, Father Joseph retained his good humor. When the ambulance rounded a turn at high speed, he commented, "This is quite a lot of fun," and when they reached the hospital he thanked the ambulance crew for "a great ride."

In the hospital Manz administered the Sacrament of the Sick. When a nurse asked Muzquiz to rate his pain on a one to ten scale, Manz was surprised to hear him rate it as six or seven because his expression remained perfectly serene. A little later, Carl Schmitt, director of the Chestnut Hill center, arrived. Schmitt had brought with him the small picture frame which Father Joseph kept in his room with pictures of the Blessed Virgin and of Escriva and the strip of paper on which Escrivá had written "Jose Luis, talk to me." When Schmitt took it out of his briefcase, Father Joseph commented, "Oh, wonderful."

Muzquiz tried to explain to Manz where he was in the classes he was giving and what the priest who took his place would have to do. When a nurse said he shouldn't try to talk, he began to write out instructions. Although normally his handwriting was very clear, the pages were illegible.

For a while Schmitt, Manz, and Dr. Bowman stayed with Muzquiz and together they made their afternoon mental prayer. When the nursing shift changed at 4:00 p.m., the new nurses insisted on enforcing the intensive care unit's strict rules about visitors, so Manz returned to Arnold Hall and Schmitt went to spend the night at Dr. Bowman's house. As Schmitt left the room, Father Joseph, whose usual parting was, "So long," raised his hand and said "God bless you, Newby, God bless you," using the nickname Schmitt's family had used for him ever since his slightly older brother had begun using it for the "new baby" in the family.

During the late afternoon and evening, Muzquiz experienced several incidents of more intense pain which were treated with morphine and other drugs. At around 2:10 a.m. the nurse noticed signs of trouble on the heart monitor and asked if he was in pain. When he said no, she teased: "I'm not sure you'd tell me if you were." "Oh yes I would," Muzquiz responded. "They told me to report any pain, and I will." He asked her to hand him the watch Escrivá had given him. "I knew it was important to him," the nurse said later, "because he did not look at the dial and a few minutes later asked me the time. He only wanted to have it close to him." The nurse lingered in the room, busying herself with small details. "I enjoyed being with him," she explained later. "You can leave now," Muzquiz said. "You must have things to do, and I'm working you like a dog."

About 2:30 a.m. he suffered another massive heart attack. The hospital staff began cardiopulmonary resuscitation. At one point, the nurse pumping Muzquiz's chest was asked if she wanted to be relieved. "No," she replied, "I want to stay here." Dr. Bowman rushed to the hospital to direct the resuscitation efforts. After some time, another doctor said, "You've done everything possible. There's no more. Would you like me to take over?" Knowing he could not bring himself to end the resuscitation efforts, Dr. Bowman made way for the other doctor, who at 3:08 a.m. pronounced Father Joseph dead.

In an unusual spontaneous gesture of affection for a patient they'd known only a few hours, two of the nurses removed all the tubes and lines rather than leaving that task for funeral home personnel. They dressed and covered Muzquiz's body with extraordinary dignity and folded his hands across his chest, with his rosary in his hands and his watch at his side. Although hardened to death by their work in the coronary unit, the nurses found their eyes filling with tears. "We've only known him a short time," they said later, "but we loved him. He was so sweet, so sweet."

At approximately 8:10 a.m. in Spain an Opus Dei priest celebrating Mass in Pamplona experienced just before the consecration a vivid "presence" of Muzquiz, something that had never happened to him before. Later that day, he learned that Father Joseph had died at just that moment. A Spanish woman who had attended some classes given by Muzquiz awoke on the morning of Tuesday, June 21 feeling especially optimistic and thinking she could achieve certain goals in her interior life. Although she normally went to confession on a different day, she decided to go to confession that morning before Mass. On her way to work, she felt an unusual degree of supernatural joy. A few hours later, she received word of Muzquiz's death.

Clad in festive white vestments, Father Joseph's body was returned to the oratory of the Chestnut Hill center where he had lived the final years of his life. During the entire night of June 21–22 he was accompanied by a stream of people who came to pray for him and to him. The next day his body was transferred to St. Aidan's church in Brookline, Massachusetts where hundreds came for the wake and for prayer throughout the night. Among the mourners were Cardinal Medeiros, the Vicar General of Boston, Bishop Thomas Dailey, a friend since the earliest days of Opus Dei in the United States, and several Boston auxiliary bishops including Bishop Lawrence Riley who had first met Muzquiz in 1949.

After the graveside ritual was over, a crowd remained at the gravesite. As the cemetery workers lowered the coffin and began to shovel dirt into the grave, a number of women dropped pieces of paper into it. Puzzled, the workers began to retrieve the papers and return them until the women stopped them.

They explained that they had written the names of friends for whom Father Joseph might intercede.

Since then Muzquiz's grave has remained a favorite spot for many visitors, including those who make pilgrimages before an image of the Blessed Mother on the tombstone. They come not only to pray for him but also to ask the intercession of a man who they feel sure is looking down on them from heaven and remains as anxious to help them as he was during his lifetime.

On learning of Muzquiz's death, Del Portillo telegraphed the members of Opus Dei in the United States asking that they pray for Muzquiz while also giving thanks to Our Lady "who has wished to bless so abundantly the silent, sacrificial, heroic work of this brother of ours and of the first ones who accompanied him in plowing the earth of that beloved country . . . for the fidelity with which he has sacrificed his life day by day, in complete union with our Father who will have welcomed him joyfully in heaven." A few days later he commented in a letter that Muzquiz had "led an exemplary life as a good son of God in Opus Dei, full of a spirit of sacrifice and of fidelity to the spirit of our Father throughout his years of work." The doctor who took care of him summed up what many people felt: Father Joseph, he said, had been "like St. John at the end of his life. Like him he was so pure, so simple, and so full of love."